We Want You to Know

We Want You to Know

Kids Talk about Bullying

DEBORAH ELLIS

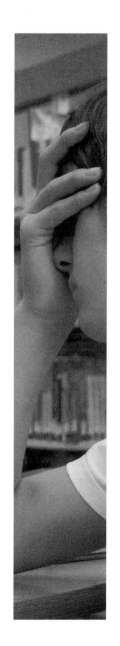

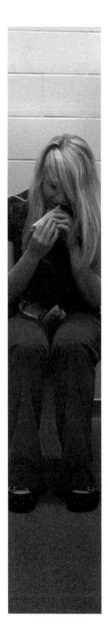

Library and Archives Canada Cataloguing in Publication

Ellis, Deborah, 1960–
We want you to know : kids talk about
bullying/Deborah Ellis

Includes index.
ISBN 978-1-55050-463-7

1. Bullying—Juvenile literature. 1. Title

BF637.B85.E47 2010   j302.3   C2010-905675-5

Library of Congress Control Number
2010935820

Available in Canada from:
Publishers Group Canada
2440 Viking Way
Richmond, BC Canada V6V 1N2

Available in the USA from:
Orca Book Publishers
www.orcabook.com
1-800-210-5277

Study Guide available free of charge from:
http://coteaubooks.com/cmsupload/fckeditor/
Study_Guides/we want you study guide.pdf

2517 Victoria Ave.
Regina, SK Canada S4P 0T2
www.coteaubooks.com

Coteau Books gratefully acknowledges the financial support of its publishing program by: the Saskatchewan Arts Board, the Canada Council for the Arts, the Government of Canada through the Canada Book Fund, the Government of Saskatchewan through the Creative Economy Entrepreneurial Fund and the City of Regina Arts Commission.

Editor: Ann Featherstone
Cover photo: Julia McAlpine
Cover and book design: Fortunato Design Inc.

All photos supplied by Julia McAlpine, with the exception of pages 14, 16, 21, 24, 33, 36, 44, 52, 57, 62, 64, 68, 72, 75, 88 and 104: the author.

Printed in Canada by Friesens
10 9 8 7 6 5 4 3 2 1

DEDICATION

To kids who seek courage with honor

We must be the change we want to see.
—MAHATMA GHANDI

CONTENTS

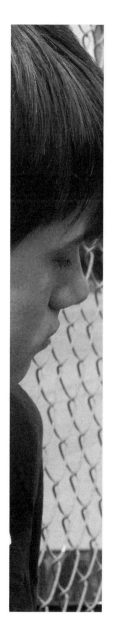

ACKNOWLEDGEMENTS

I'd like to thank the children and families who shared their stories with me, my colleagues at Haldimand-Norfolk REACH, the Ontario Trillium Foundation, the Canadian International School in Tokyo, Raising Voices Uganda, and the international school in Antananarivo, Madagascar. And, of course, Ann Featherstone, my editor.

The snapshots of the children interviewed were taken by me, but the background photos were taken by a talented young photographer, Julia McAlpine, with the assistance of friends and teachers at Holy Trinity High School in Simcoe, Ontario, Canada.

Royalties from the sale of this book will go to the
Name It 2 Change It Community Campaign Against Bullying.

www.nameit2changeit.ca

INTRODUCTION

IN MY OTHER BOOKS, I have looked at the effects of global bullying on people around the world—people who are the victims of war or poverty, and people who've experienced the fallout from war and poverty, such as AIDS, the illegal drug trade, and prison.

This book is about bullying on a more personal level.

The Name It 2 Change It Campaign was initiated by a community anti-bullying committee as a means to respond to the increasing amount of bullying and its effects in Haldimand, Norfolk, and neighboring communities in Southern Ontario. Through my association with the campaign and my job as a community organizer for them, I interviewed kids from the ages of nine to nineteen, and I asked them to talk about their experiences.

In this book, you'll meet kids who have been bullied, kids who have bullied others, and kids who have found the strength within themselves to rise above their situations and to endure.

There is more than one side to every story. Many kids talked about how teachers in their school seem to do nothing to stop their tormentors. I know that teachers do a lot, but rules of confidentiality prevent them from sharing information about all their efforts. But somehow we must find a way to show the victims of bullying that they are being heard.

All the kids interviewed in this book come from my little corner of Southern Ontario. This is a lovely part of a lovely country, and if bullying is happening here, then it's happening everywhere. Some kids chose to use their real first name and photo. Some kids chose to tell their story under a pseudonym without a photo. All kids made these decisions with the participation and permission of their parents. These are kids who responded to a call I put out, or who were referred to me by teachers and colleagues.

Although I asked some standard questions, such as, "What happened to you," "How did you respond," and "How did you

feel," most of the interviews were directed by the kids themselves. When they told me things they later asked me to delete, I respected their wishes.

These kids spoke quite candidly about what they've gone through and what they have learned from their experiences. They've shown courage in speaking out, and I honor them.

The additional comments from kids around the world are excerpts from essays they wrote about bullying. Their words show that this is an issue that does not stop at national borders.

PART ONE

YOU'RE NOT GOOD ENOUGH

THOSE WHO BULLY OTHERS often provide excuses for their behavior, excuses that give them permission, in their own minds, to treat someone else badly.

All of us are excluded from some groups, and sometimes for valid reasons. If a group forms a chess club, it makes sense to exclude kids who can't or won't learn to play chess. If you want to join an orchestra, you're required to play an instrument. If you want to join a hockey team, you'll have to know how to play the game.

Some groups are designed to exclude others for no particular reason at all. They are formed in order to make their members feel superior to others. They have no special abilities or interests. And their definition of "good enough" always changes.

The kids interviewed in this section have been excluded because someone else or a group has decided they don't measure up.

KATIE, 16

I'VE LIVED IN THIS AREA ALL MY LIFE. I now live a little ways out in the country, between two small towns.

I was homeschooled until grade seven. My mother started homeschooling with my brother, and it went really well, so she kept it up with me. We got courses from an American Christian correspondence school, and that's what we learned from. You have to be self-disciplined for homeschooling to work well.

When it was time for me to start grade seven, I wanted to go to a regular school, to see what it was like. Also, my mom was running a day-care center at our house, and I wanted a break from all the little kids. My parents took some convincing—they were happy with the way things were—but they finally relented because I wouldn't stop bugging them.

I started classes a week after the school year began, going to a middle school that was only grade seven and eight. I was excited to be there, even though I didn't know anyone.

I wanted so badly to make friends. That's supposed to be the fun part of school, isn't it? But the other girls wouldn't include me. They'd all known each other forever, and they didn't need me or try to get to know me.

There was one girl I thought was becoming friends with me, and I gave her a friendship charm. Two days later, she gave it back to me with a note that said she had enough friends and didn't need me. It was a mean note. It surprised me, because I hadn't been mean to her. I went home and cried.

The whole year would have been easier if they'd just included me, but that never happened. Instead, they started actively excluding me. They'd go out of their way to let me know they didn't want me around.

They'd hide my gym bag when it was time for gym so that I'd get into trouble with the teacher. Afterward I'd hear them laughing about it. Or they'd stop talking when I walked by them, then laugh at my back as I walked away. A girl I sat on the school bus with had a birthday party. She made a big show of handing out party invitations to all the girls in the class—except me. In the change room one time, a girl slapped me on the head—out of the blue, for no reason—then just laughed and went back to changing her clothes. I remember how badly my ear burned where she hit me. I thought I was going to go deaf, the pain was so bad. But, of course, I never tattled.

I stayed all year at the school, but it never got any better. I thought that once I stopped being new and they got used to me, they'd calm down, get to know and accept me. But that never happened. One girl would pretend to like me when she was fighting with her real friends. But when they made up, she'd go back to trashing me again.

I went back to being homeschooled in grade eight. I didn't want to go through another year of being shut out. I didn't want to be around those people anymore. And they certainly didn't want me around, so they got their wish. It was such a relief the day after Labor Day that year, when everyone else went back to school and I got to stay home. I thought about all those girls looking for me, thinking up new ways to make me unhappy—and me not being there. I hope they were disappointed.

My parents wanted me to go back to regular school for high school. They wanted me to have access to more courses, and to a Canadian curriculum, which, of course, is different from the American curriculum I'd been studying through correspondence. They told me high school would be better than grade seven; and so far, it is. There are more kids and it's easier to stay away from someone you want to avoid. Plus, we're all getting older and hopefully more mature.

I can't say I actually like high school, but there are some good things about it. Mrs. Douglas, our Food and Nutrition teacher, has a part of her class time she calls Community Circle, where we all just talk about things. She starts us off talking about easy things—like our favorite foods. It's surprising how often an easy topic will help us feel comfortable talking about harder things, like life and relationships.

I'm still not popular, but it doesn't bother me. I have a few friends—other misfits!—and I work at the public library. I love old movies, especially musicals. I hope to be a film historian one day.

I think I've learned from this experience to give a newcomer a chance. Just because you've hung out with the same people forever doesn't mean that someone new coming along won't also add to your life. But you'll never know unless you give them a chance and find out who they are.

WHAT DO YOU THINK?

- Are there ways parents can help to prepare their children for the social challenges they might face at school?

- How could the other students have made Katie feel more welcome?

If you and other people in your class are bullied, you can help each other out. You will get more friends and feel better. This is my advice. You don't have to listen to it, but I think you should.

-BIRGIT SALOMONSEN DYGARD,
GRADE FIVE, MADAGASCAR

CARL, 13

I HAVE ONE CAT here at my mom's, and one cat and two dogs at my dad's. I'm a big animal person.

Bullying started to become part of my life in grade six and grew worse in grade seven. Kids started making fun of my height, my laugh, how I did things, what I did. Before grade six, it didn't happen.

New people came into the school, and I think they chose to try to fit in by making other kids feel on the outside. These new kids changed the behavior of the kids I'd always gone to school with. Some of these kids were my good friends.

My friends made friends with the new kids and picked up from the new kids that I wasn't wanted. So, bit by bit, they started treating me the way the new kids were treating me. They started picking on me, too.

I was kind of surprised by that. No one had really picked on me before. I wasn't really a person to pick on, so it wasn't something I'd had to deal with before.

I didn't respond to a lot of it. Sometimes I did, but that didn't make it stop. I didn't really know what to do.

It started in the middle of grade six. At first, it seemed like good-natured teasing, the sort of things kids do. But it changed into something else. It got bigger and bigger. They knew I didn't like it because I told them, and that just made them do it more. I felt mad and sad, and I didn't know what to do.

I told my mom about a few things, but not very much. I didn't say anything to the teachers because I thought if I told them, they wouldn't do anything. Maybe they'd say one or two things just to be able to say they'd done something, but they wouldn't really do anything.

One teacher at my school didn't overly like me. I'd raise my hand and she'd ignore me. It happened a lot, and I guessed it was because she didn't like me. I don't know why. I thought if they didn't overly like me, then they wouldn't want to believe me, and things would just get worse.

My old friends might have seen on their own that their new friends were bullying me, but if they did, they didn't show any signs of it. Most of the bullying didn't happen in front of them.

Generally it happened outside during recess. The bullies would go to other people and point at me and laugh and say bad stuff about me. They'd say these things loud enough so I could hear them. I guess they didn't care what I thought, but in some ways, they did, because they wanted me to feel bad. I've experienced that bullies want to see anger coming out of you. They want to see you frustrated, and they want you to feel lower. I tried not to let them make me feel bad, but I just really couldn't.

One reason those hurtful messages got into my head was I felt the teachers wouldn't understand. I thought they might even suspend me or something. I didn't think the teachers were on my side, so I felt very lonely and very alone. I didn't know what to do.

I didn't have anyone to turn to. Then my parents got divorced, and I moved with my dad and went to a new school. This was a grade seven and eight school. I was in grade seven. I had friends for the first couple of days, and then I guess they lost interest in me and shut me out.

Then they heard me laughing at something one day and said my laugh was weird and stupid. They said it over and over again, on and on, even when I asked them not to. Why make fun of my laugh?

They started with my laugh, and then moved on to my height, what I did, and how I did it. I wasn't doing anything particularly strange, but they always found something to criticize about me. It was all to tell me that I wasn't worth as much as them, that I wasn't as good as they were.

I spoke to my French teacher about it. She spoke to the kids who were going after me, but it didn't change anything.

I don't know how I found the strength to keep going to school every day. I just focused on my schoolwork and tried not to let things get to me.

Schoolwork has always been a struggle for me, but I found that when I concentrate, I can get through it. All this stuff going on at school made it really hard to concentrate. I never knew when the next assault would come.

I really like art, especially drawing cartoons. I draw little characters and faces. It brightens me up to do this. It's comical. It's funny. I've learned that work is a good thing to focus on when life gets hard.

This year is better because I have a new friend. We hang out all the time. We both like video games and art. He does cartooning as well, and some other kinds of drawing.

When my old friends teamed up with the guys who were bullying me, I felt really betrayed. I felt lonely.

It kind of added to my stress at the time that my parents were going through a divorce, but it kind of didn't at the same time. There are lots of kids whose parents are divorced. I tried to do what they did, because they didn't seem to get picked on. The other things that are going on in my life shouldn't affect the way people are treating me.

Like, some days I felt sad because my dad wasn't around. Some days I went to school slouchy and stuff, and then people would comment on that, and I wouldn't say anything because I didn't want to talk about it. Then they'd keep on bugging me and bugging me. They wouldn't give me my space and respect. They'd just use it as another reason to go after me.

Through all this, I've learned a lot about what I need to be happy. I've also learned a bit about how to get that for myself no matter what else is going on around me. I've learned that I'm someone who likes to have at least one close friend, not someone who needs to have a whole lot of friends. And I've learned that art is something that I'll always have, and no kids being jerks can take that from me.

About other people, I've learned that bullies are often people who haven't been treated nicely in the past. They find someone who used to be happy, the same way they used to be, and they pick on them until everybody feels bad and down.

I can stand up for myself better now because I have at least one friend who will never turn on me the way my old friends did. Even when he goes to make new friends, he won't turn on me. We have lots of fun, lots of things in common. He's just one of those friends that you know you'll never have to worry about.

WHAT DO YOU THINK?

- Carl uses his talent as an artist to build himself up when others try to make him feel bad. What do you use?

- Through his experience with bullying, Carl has learned what he needs to do to be happy. What do you need to be happy? What about the others in your family—what do they need?

EMILY, 13

I CAN'T CONNECT with my friends anymore. It's such a small school and everyone hangs around in groups, and I just can't connect with them.

They've changed, and I've changed. They like pop music, and I like rock and roll. I like to draw, and they don't.

The school is so small there are only nine girls in my class. Five of them have always been in a group of their own, a group that I've never belonged to. The other four of us used to be friends.

Now I'm on my own. That would be okay if the teacher didn't keep putting us in groups for projects. She means well, but it's very awkward for me now. If I say something to her, she might let me work on my own. That would be easier. It's lonelier, but sometimes being lonely is the better way to go.

We were all pretty close in grade seven, but at the start of grade eight it seemed like they'd changed. It got worse over time. They'd leave me out of conversations.

I'm just naturally quiet, and I've learned to keep to myself. It helps that I'm close to my brother. He's eighteen, and after a rotten day at school I can come home and play video games with him and feel better.

He tells me I'll meet a lot of new people in high school, and I shouldn't let the girls in grade eight bother me. After all, he says, grade eight doesn't last forever.

All of this has changed my feelings about school. I used to like it. Now I've got half the year still to go, and I don't know how I'll get through it. It just feels so lonely.

Sometimes my mom lets me stay home. She says, "You can stay home today if you really need a break, but the problem will still be there waiting for you tomorrow." Sometimes it's nice to have a break. It doesn't fix anything, but it lets you catch your breath.

One of the girls is really good at getting everyone else to go along with her opinions. So when you get on the bad side of her, it's very, very difficult. She becomes very whiney if she doesn't get her way.

I don't think the teachers see this as bullying. The principal says she doesn't want to take sides when I try to tell her about it, and my teacher thinks everyone is getting along just fine.

It takes me a long time to make friends, so when I fell out of the group, I felt I had no place to go. I'm alone there.

My older sister had a good experience at her school. The teacher and the principal took bullying very seriously. They even brought in the police. My sister was cyber-bullied. That's why the police were brought in, because it's illegal to use the Internet to bully someone.

My sister has a close friend who's a girl. So some girls decided my sister and her friend were lesbians and put that up on the Internet. It got around everywhere.

My sister and her friend ignored it for as long as they could. There's nothing wrong with being a lesbian—some people are; some people aren't. My sister and her friend didn't want to make a big deal out of it. They hoped it would all go away, but it didn't, and it kept building. So they went to their principal. The principal called the police, and they said to the kids who started it, "This stops now or we will charge you."

Now she's friends with those girls again. The ones who spread the rumor apologized and listened to her tell them how she felt about what they did. And they repaired the damage they had done to their friendship. So it had a good ending. But while it was happening, she cried all the time and never got a full night's sleep.

I'd find going to school easier if my old friends weren't there. I can't get away from them. I need to go out into the bigger world and meet new people, but I'm stuck in this school until the end of grade eight.

I'm the sort of person who holds a lot in. For the longest time I didn't tell my parents what was going on. Then one day I was all ready for school, got to the door, and started crying. And that's when we started talking about it.

Probably the only way I'll get through the next few months is to focus on the things I enjoy, like drawing. I'll draw and do my work, and wait for the year to pass.

WHAT DO YOU THINK?

- Is there something the teachers can do in Emily's case, or should they leave the girls to sort it out on their own?

- What do you think of Emily's strategy to keep to herself and wait for grade nine for things to change? What are the pros and cons of that strategy?

ADAM, 10

I'VE BEEN PUSHED, shoved, hit, and called names. It's been going on for two years. I hate going to school now.

When I was in grade three, I got glasses, and kids started teasing me by calling me "four eyes." That wasn't nice, but I could handle it. I mean, it hurt my feelings, but it got worse in the older grades. It got physical.

There're five guys who beat me up all the time. They are in the same grade as I am. It usually happens at recess when the teacher isn't looking. There are only two teachers on yard duty when all the kids are out there, and they can't see everything.

They go after me because they think I'm weak. Since I have glasses, they think they are tougher than I am.

When they attack me, it happens out of the blue. We're not in an argument. They just see me and decide to pound or push me.

Sometimes they threaten me. One of them said, "I'm going to bring a knife to school tomorrow and cut you up." Another time, they said, "We've all decided to beat you up after school today, so get ready to be hurt."

Two days ago, it was Sunday. I was sitting beside my mom in church. This one kid from the gang was sitting two rows in front of us. He turned around and swore at me and made swear words with his hands. When we were walking down to Sunday school, he got beside me and called me names and said that on Monday they were all going to beat me up at school.

I told the principal on Monday, and she said, "Many times you have lied, Adam, so why should I believe you now?"

I tell the teachers and the principal, but nothing gets better. Sometimes someone in the gang gets suspended, but they just laugh and say, "Holiday!"

Sometimes the teachers tell me, "If you don't want to get beat up, stay inside for recess."

At least my parents believe me, and I have a couple of friends who see it happen. We stand together, but it isn't always enough. The gang just likes bullying! They like to get people to show emotion. If they make somebody cry, they laugh and say, "I just won!"

My mom tries to help. She calls the school and she calls the principal, but the principal doesn't believe her, even! The principal will say, "You can't prove Adam was hurt on school property, so there's nothing we can do about it."

I have bruises a lot. One time I was shoved so hard to the ground they thought my nose was broken.

I'm really tired of it. I want to feel safe at school. I want to just do my work sheets and get good marks on them again. When I sit at my desk I always worry that one of the gang will call me names when the teacher isn't paying attention, so I think about that instead of my work. My grades are not so good anymore.

I come home from school and I feel angry and can't relax. My mom knows when I've had a bad day because she says I take my anger out on my sister and I look really sad.

The way I make myself happy again is to look forward to growing up, to getting my driver's license, and buying a farm. I'm going to be a farmer. That makes me happy.

WHAT DO YOU THINK?

- What is making it difficult for the teachers to be sympathetic to Adam?

- If you were in Adam's situation, what could you do to get the teachers' attention? If they can't help, what else can you do?

Bullying makes you feel threatened. It damages your emotions, leaving a scar in your heart forever. I have been bullied and I would like to tell you not to be afraid of a bully. Be brave and stand up for yourself, and make them feel that you are not weak.

–KIM WOO LEE,
GRADE SEVEN, SINGAPORE

MILLIE, 14

I'm not sure when the bullying started—grade three or four, maybe. It was mostly in grade four and five, and it went on into secondary school, on and off.

I was excluded from my friends. They'd be talking and I'd come up and they'd go quiet. They'd tease me. At first it was joking-teasing, but then it got more serious and they wouldn't stop, even when I asked them to.

They'd be talking about me behind my back, telling little jokes about me. They'd do this to a few people.

It was a weird sort of a game they were playing. Like, a whole recess would go by and no one would talk to me. These girls were all my friends, and sometimes they'd be friendly and include me. Other times, all of a sudden, no one would talk to me and I'd be left standing alone on the playground. I never knew from recess to recess what would happen. It felt out of my control, and I'd dread recess.

Sometimes I'd go and hang out with other girls, girls I hadn't really hung out with before, but that felt awkward. I felt like they knew I was being shunned by my friends and were only talking to me out of pity. I don't know if that was true or not, but that's what I felt.

It was around this time that I really got into reading. I'd take a book out to recess and find a place to sit by myself.

When I look back on it, I think it was deliberate. I'd go out for recess, look for my friends, see them, and head toward them. They'd see me, then they'd turn and walk away. Or they'd start running around and completely ignore me.

When they'd tease me, it was about my appearance. I hit puberty early and had bad acne when no one else did. I got my period in grade four, and the whole thing was really new to me. My mom told me what to expect, of course, but you don't really know until you go through it. So I went to the teacher when no one else was in the classroom and told him I had my period and might have to go to the bathroom more than I normally would. He said, okay, no problem, you don't even have to ask, just go.

But apparently someone was walking by and overheard, and they twisted it completely and spread it all over the school. So that was another reason I wanted to keep to myself.

I try not to think about those days too much. I don't know why they behaved like that since we'd been really good friends up until then. I tried to talk to them about it a couple of times, but they just said, "Oh, we were just teasing—can't you take a joke?"

People can change, though. Kids who used to tease me became my friends. A lot of them came to my thirteenth birthday. My mom and I talk a lot about how we don't always know what we're doing when we're young, and when we get older, we make better decisions. So you should never give up hope. If you're in a terrible situation now, it can change and get better.

WHAT DO YOU THINK?

- What could Millie say or do when her friends are friendly one day and unfriendly the next?

- Do you agree with Millie and her mom that we don't always know what we're doing when we're young?

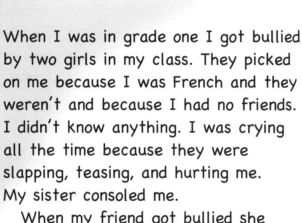

When I was in grade one I got bullied by two girls in my class. They picked on me because I was French and they weren't and because I had no friends. I didn't know anything. I was crying all the time because they were slapping, teasing, and hurting me. My sister consoled me.

When my friend got bullied she was crying and I consoled her. Before that, she wasn't my friend, but that is why we are friends now.
–Beryl Dabezies,
GRADE FIVE, MADAGASCAR

MEGAN, 12

I've always gone to the same school. It's a small country school. My town is more country than town.

It's generally a good school, but things started to change with the girls when I got into grade six.

Some girls formed the Blonde Girls Club. It started with four blondes, but then another one came, and that's when they formed their club. They do things together and don't include the Brunettes.

We formed the Brunette Club so that we can fight back because they are always so rude to us. I have four friends. Three are brunettes and one is a blonde. She went over to the Blonde Club and started being mean to us. They'd gossip about us and wouldn't let us play with them. They'd tell us our clothes were ugly and our shoes were terrible.

I told them they weren't being nice. There's a saying: What you say is what you are. So if you say someone else's shoes are ugly, really you're saying your shoes are ugly.

They were kind of speechless when I said that. I guess they didn't expect anyone to stand up to them, so they didn't know what to say.

The Blonde Club thinks that having blonde hair makes them special. They got this idea from a new girl who came and wanted to take over things. Some kids seem to need another kid to lead them, so when a stronger kid comes and says they should do bad things, they'll fall in line because that makes them feel stronger and important, too.

The Blonde Club made me unhappy because it felt like people were changing, and not in good ways. We are a small school, so small changes feel like something really big. So when my friends stopped being my friends because they started to believe that blonde hair is better, it really hurt my feelings. The color of your hair doesn't say anything about who you are. That comes from your brain and your heart.

It wasn't fair that the Blondes wouldn't let the Brunettes play with them. The Blondes thought they'd be less cool if they played with the Brunettes.

I never believed I wasn't cool because I'm a brunette. Everybody's cool, really, in their own way. Sometimes the Blondes would put me down or ignore me, and that would really hurt because I wasn't doing anything to them. My parents would try to cheer me up, but I couldn't just go to them all the time. I have to learn to take care of my own problems and stand up for myself.

I guess I did let what they said bother me and get under my skin. It bothered my friends, too.

Sometimes the Blondes would bother us too much. They'd tease us and bug us and laugh at our hair, over and over and over again. They would take it right to the limit, where we would start thinking that we should move somewhere else to get away from them.

When I started trusting myself and believing in my friends, everything changed. I started standing up for myself. My friends were by my side and it helped me to gain more confidence. If one of my friends was in trouble, I'd stand up for her, and that made me feel good, too.

If a kid is having mother-and-father problems, it's harder for her to stand up for herself because she is so worried. Like, if she has a sick parent, or if her parents are always fighting or getting divorced, the kid has to spend so much energy worrying about them that she has no energy left to stand up for herself. And that's when some kids will swoop down and really start to bully her because they know she won't fight back.

I'm very lucky to have good friends. We help each other get through things. And I have good parents.

We have a religious grotto at our school, out by the back forty. My friends and I like to hang out there at recess because it's such a nice place. It's sort of our space, but we don't keep anyone out.

When the Blonde Club was going on, the teachers got all the girls involved to have a Girl Talk, to talk about what was going on, and to try to find solutions. The Blonde Club got mad that we had told on them, but I think it was good to talk about it and get it out in the open.

I think the Blondes still bug us sometimes because they are bored. They can't think of anything else to do.

Generally, it's a really nice school, and people treat each other well. I think we will be able to put all this club stuff behind us, and just get to know each other as kids. The girls in the Blonde Club have a lot of good qualities, and one day, we'll get to be friends.

I don't know what I want to do with my life. Mostly I don't want anything really bad to happen. And I'd like to be a dress designer. I like drawing designs for new dresses.

My parents help a lot by encouraging me and helping me come up with solutions to my problems.

WHAT DO YOU THINK?

- Why do you think the blonde girls formed the Blonde Club?

- What do you think of Megan and her friends' idea to form their own club? What might be the positive and negative sides to that idea?

SERENA, 12

I started being bullied at the end of grade five, and now it's gotten to the point where it's, like, crazy.

There is one girl at school who is behind it. She's cyber-bullied me—written bad stuff about me on the Internet, about kicking me out of her group—and she gossips about me. I hear from the other girls about all the bad things she says about me.

I met her in kindergarten. We were best friends in grade four and five. At the end of grade five she said she didn't want to be my friend anymore. But when we were in soccer together, she sort of forgot about us not being friends. Then, after soccer was over, she said again that we were done being friends, and that's when the bullying started.

I'm not the only one she targets. She wrote nasty comments on one boy's Facebook page, and everyone

I talk to about her says, "Oh, she's so mean!" It's lots of little things that don't seem like big deals when I try to talk about them, but they add up. Like, when we're in choir and she says hi to all the others but not to me.

We had to do a project in math class where we made envelopes (we were studying angles) and I needed tape, which was on her desk. It was the classroom tape, not her personal tape. I went over and said to her, "Okay, I need this." But she got up, took the tape, and carried it to the other side of the classroom.

Another time, we were in the change room getting dressed after gym class. She had a bottle of body spray, like a perfume, and all the other girls wanted to try it, so she gave everyone a spray except me.

She's nice to other people sometimes, and she'll exclude me, really making a point of keeping me out.

She's the kind of person others will follow because she has lots of confidence. Some people aren't so confident, so they'll latch onto people who are strong because it's easier for them to follow than to be on their own. Also, people will try hard to stay her friend so she doesn't get mad at them, because if she gets mad, she'll start bullying. People don't want to stand up to her. When she gets mad, she'll turn everyone else against the one person she specifically gets mad at.

It's nothing physical or verbal. It's nothing you can go to a teacher and say, "This is what she did to me," because her way of bullying isn't exactly break- ing any rules. Well, except for the cyber-bullying.

I told my parents about it. They said, at first, "Oh, you'll be best friends again by next week." Well, we weren't. And I'm not expecting to be best friends again because, seeing the other side of her, I know she's not someone I'd want to be best friends with.

One day I was sitting at my desk at lunchtime. Everyone else was hanging around her desk. My teacher came up to me and asked, "Are you feeling okay?" and I said, "Yeah." Then she asked, "Are you having friend problems?" I said, "Yeah," so she asked me to come out into the hall and talk with her. I did, and in the hall I started crying and told her what was happening.

She brought us together at recess to discuss it. I appreciate that she did that. She took it seriously and she tried to help. It didn't really change anything, but I felt better knowing that I was heard. It was also nice of her to come up and ask me what was wrong, rather than wait for me to say something.

I know a girl who had to change schools because of this girl. If you're not strong, it can make you feel very alone, and it can make you doubt yourself. You start to wonder if anyone will ever like you again, and you start to wonder what's wrong with you that you're being treated this way.

It made me feel uncomfortable to go to school because I was worried I'd say something that would make this girl get mad and bully me worse.

My mom phoned her mom and said, "Okay, your daughter's getting really mean to mine." Her mom talked to her, then this girl came to school angry at me because I'd gotten her mom on her back.

It all really bothered me. I wouldn't be able to sleep at night because I was so worried. I'd be angry all the time at home and pick fights with my brother and sister. I stayed away from any activity where this girl might be—at church and at school.

I used to be afraid of her becoming angry at me, but I'm not anymore. It's like she has no more power over me. It's a good feeling. She used to bother me so much that it affected my schoolwork; I couldn't concentrate properly. But things are much better now.

I feel bad that we're not friends anymore, but it's also a relief that I don't have to come to school every day and try to make someone feel like they're the queen. When I look back on our friendship now, I was often worried that I'd do something to upset her. It wasn't relaxing, the way friendship is supposed to be. So now I feel free.

I suppose she could still hurt me, but I don't care anymore whether she likes me or not, so she won't be able to hurt me too much. And not being friends with her anymore has left me with time to get to know other kids, and I'm friends now with some really nice girls.

It still makes me mad that she's bullied other kids for such a long time. Maybe she'll grow out of it. I've got two more years at this school with her, but I can handle it. If it keeps happening, my parents will take it to the school board. We've also been told by the police that bullying should be taken seriously.

At the last meeting we had to resolve this, the principal made us write on little pieces of paper how we'll move forward. And then we're going to go back to her office this week and burn the pieces of paper. She said, "Once we burn these, it's going to become a part of us." I don't really get it, but what the heck, maybe it will help. I try to have an open mind. She's suggested other things that are great, like she gave me a set of faith cards to read, one each day, and I know that I am a special gift from God. And she asked me to help with the Beatitudes Banner that we're going to hang up in the library.

I try to keep myself well and happy and strong no matter what this girl does. Like, I stopped eating lunch in the classroom. I go and volunteer in the kindergarten room to get away from her, and that makes me happier.

I don't know what this girl is thinking. Maybe she's lonely. Her mom says she has come home from school crying, too, because people don't want to be her friends. So maybe she tries to control people because she thinks they won't hang out with her by their own choice. I don't know. It's not my problem to solve.

I have lots of great things in my life, and the great things outnumber the difficult things.

WHAT DO YOU THINK?

- Why was Serena so hurt even though she was not the only person to be bullied by this girl?

- Do you agree with Serena when she says, "It's not my problem to solve"? Whose problem is it?

Talking About

YOU'RE NOT GOOD ENOUGH

The kids in this section talked about being excluded—left out of groups or shut out of friendships. This makes them feel sad, lonely, and stressed, and they start to believe they are not worth as much as the others. The kids who get excluded seem to be chosen randomly. Any kid could be the next one to be excluded.

- How easy is it for new kids to fit in at your school?

- How have you changed as you've gotten older? How have your friendships changed? Has this been easy to manage, or awkward?

- Have you ever felt excluded? How did you deal with it?

- Have you ever excluded someone from a group you belong to?

- How did you feel when you were excluded and when you excluded others? What did you learn from that experience?

- What can you do if you see people being excluded at your school?

- What is the difference between excluding someone and simply wanting to hang out with your best friends?

When I was younger, there was a group of kids that went around together. The leader of the group always bullied me and my friends. She made fun of our names and made fun of us when we couldn't do something in PE or in class. The kids in this group kicked us and hit us, but we couldn't say anything because we were all so scared. As we got older, they would steal my friends and say bad things about me. One day, the leader of the bullies asked me to bully someone else with her. Because I was so scared I just said, "Okay." I now understand that bullies are not brave all by themselves; they need other people around them. I don't want to be this bully's puppet anymore but it is hard to say no to someone you are scared of.

–HEA JIN JO,

GRADE FIVE, SOUTH KOREA

PART TWO

YOU'RE TOO DIFFERENT

THE WORLD IS FULL of differences. Although we all share the same needs—wanting to be happy, wanting to be safe, wanting to do work that has meaning, wanting to love and be loved—we also have many things that set us apart from one another.

Sometimes these differences are celebrated. We can learn from and respect people who see the world differently from us without feeling as if our own point of view has been threatened.

Sometimes, we use these differences as an excuse to attack each other.

Bullying will look for any excuse to justify itself.

KEISHA, 12

I've always gone to the same school, and it's generally been a good place. I've only had one problem there, and it happened a few years ago. A boy in my class started it. He and I used to be friends, but one day I was walking home from school with my dad, and this boy's dad came out with him. Our two dads got into a fight, and after that, things changed between me and this boy. He wasn't nice to me anymore, and he started to pick on me.

A few times I'd ask him to please stop it, but he wouldn't. He'd tease me and call me fat. He'd do this when he was alone, so it wasn't like he had a group of friends telling him to do it. He just decided to do it on his own.

It made me feel really bad about myself. I tried to avoid him. I'd stay with my own friends and try to stay far from him.

My friends asked him to stop, too. They didn't think he was being nice, and they could see it bothered me. It was really getting on my nerves.

It took a long time for him to stop. I think he eventually stopped because I started ignoring him, but I don't know for sure because we never talked about it.

It made me feel very bad about myself. It changed the way I saw myself because up until then I didn't think too much about how I looked. I was busy think-ing about other things, and that was fine. But then he started calling me these names and saying bad things about how I looked, and I started to worry about it.

I'd come home from school upset and crying about it. Mom is really strong and did a lot to encourage me. She said if things got worse, she would deal with it with the boy's parents, but we all know how that can some-times make things even worse. I was glad it didn't come to that. Mom was also thinking of pulling me out of the school and enrolling me in a new one. But I have friends where I am and I like the teachers, so I'm glad I didn't have to move.

I have really good friends. They helped me by say-ing good things about me. And it sort of helped that I wasn't the only one being picked on by this boy. I'd see him going after other kids and think, "Well, he can't be right about all of us, so maybe he's not right about me."

It helps when teachers get involved at school. Sometimes that's all it takes for some kids to stop, when they realize a teacher knows they're hurting someone. So kids shouldn't be afraid to go to the teachers for help. Sometimes the teachers can't do much because the parents are bullies, too, but we should at least trust them to try.

I'm a pretty strong kid. I have a strong family and strong friends, and we're all strong together. We'll never bully others because we know how it feels.

WHAT DO YOU THINK?

- When Keisha talks about the strength her family and friends give her, what do you think she means?

- Why do you think *fat* is such a powerful word?

Bullies offend our pride and hurt our feelings. It ruins our self-esteem. It's hard to shield yourself from harsh comments. This doesn't mean it's impossible, though. Always remember that you are better because you are not the one who is bullying.

–AYAN MARSHED,
GRADE THREE, CALIFORNIA

CRYSTAL, 19

I WAS DIAGNOSED with mild ataxic cerebral palsy. My teachers knew about this, but they were mainly the ones bullying me.

I'd get bullied and made fun of by kids, too, but it hurt more when the teachers did it.

I'd have trouble finishing my work on time, so, as punishment, the teachers would *post* me. Posting means I'd have to stand by a metal post all through recess. I was always there. It seemed like every recess, when I should have been having some fun, they'd make me stand by the post.

I had to miss a class party at school, too, because I wasn't able to finish my work. The party went on without me, and I had to sit in the hall to do my work.

I'd had all the medical tests done. The teachers knew what was up with me. They knew I went to special classes during the day, but it was still too much for me. I stayed up late every night, trying to learn so they wouldn't be angry. But it didn't help.

The other kids would see me on post every day, and it gave them another reason to laugh at me. They'd also run by me and play around me as if I wasn't even there—as if I was invisible.

I dealt with it every day. At the time, I had no voice. I didn't know how to speak up for myself. And I never told my parents. I figured it was my fault.

In grade six I changed schools, and things got better. They didn't have posting at this new school. I had an educational assistant to help me. When the EA was around, kids either left me alone or were kind to me. When the EA wasn't there, the kids could be mean.

I had a friend at that school who also had difficulties. The kids made fun of both of us. They were jerks. They had no understanding of who we were.

High school was a mix. I was mostly in a non-regular class—with other kids who had difficulties—and that was nice. Everyone there treated everyone else well.

In grade eleven I had some regular classes. Kids there were good and bad; the teachers were good and bad. I had a friend in a regular class who helped me a lot. We sat next to each other, and she helped me understand and do my work.

The teacher in my art class was wonderful, but there were a lot of mean girls in that class. They made fun of me and laughed at my mistakes. I was supposed to partner with one of these girls, but she refused to work with me, so I just did the project on my own. To heck with her, I thought.

I finally graduated from high school not long ago. Now I am a member of the Self-Advocates Committee. We're a committee of people with similar struggles. We go into schools and talk about bullying. We put together a very funny musical puppet show, and filmed it for DVD, called *Same Difference*.* It's to teach younger kids that we're all different and we're all the same.

We do all kinds of things. We have Shout-Outs, where folks can come from all over to talk about human rights.

We do practical things, too, to make it easier for others and to educate people. At the local fall fair, we do educational projects, see concerts, and have fun. Some of us are in wheelchairs, so we'd go in a wheelchair van. Sometimes the parking attendant would give us a hard time because she could see that some of us could walk. She'd want us to explain our disabilities, to prove that we should be able to park in a certain place. "Are you all handicapped in there?" she asked. We had a disability permit. We shouldn't have had to explain that sometimes people have trouble walking even if they're not in a wheelchair. So we all wrote a letter to the fair board and got a better place to park, for us and for others with difficulties. If it happened to us, it was happening to others. Little things like parking closer to the action at a fair means the difference between a happy time and a time when you are worn out just from crossing the parking lot.

It's important to contribute to the community, to volunteer and to try to make things better. You can take what's happened to you and be bitter, or you can learn from it and help others. You have to live your life and have fun.

If you see someone being bullied, stand up for them. It will make you feel good.

If you are being bullied, know that you are not alone. There are people out there who will help you. Don't stop looking until you find them, because you are worth it.

*For a copy of the DVD *Same Difference*, contact Community Living Haldimand by phone: 1-905-772-3344 or by e-mail: centraladmin@clhaldimand.com

WHAT DO YOU THINK?

• Crystal talks about doing practical things to make it easier for others. What are some practical things you can do in your community?

• Crystal talks about us all being different and the same. What do you think she means by this?

PATRICIA, 12 and SARAH, 10—Sisters

PATRICIA

I LIKE SCHOOL, but I sometimes have a difficult time there. I have an EA—an educational assistant—so some kids think that I don't matter.

I have good days and bad days at school. Even when I was very young, in grade one, this bullying was going on. A teacher in grade one used to be really mean to me because I wasn't like the other kids.

Kids, too, were mean to me. All through school, stuff has happened to me. To my sister, too. I don't know why they pick on us. We're nice people and we don't deserve to be bullied.

Sometimes the bullying is kids just leaving me out, ignoring me, and making me feel that I'm not good enough to be with them.

I've had friends, too. I've had good times at school as well as bad times. But my friends have come and gone. They move to different schools.

Just the other day, some girls called me a loser, told me that I was ugly, that I was trying to be like them because they were cool. I don't think it's cool to try to be like someone else. It's cooler to try to be yourself. They ripped up my things. They flushed my lip gloss down the toilet.

Sometimes when these things happen, I'll tell a teacher that someone has hurt me. But when the teacher talks to the kid who bullied me, then the kid gets mad and I'm back in trouble with them. More bullying. And sometimes the teacher doesn't believe me. I got punched in the face once in the school yard and got a black eye from it. I told the teacher and she said I probably did it to myself.

Sometimes if they hit me first, I'd hit them back, but if I was the one caught doing the hitting, then I'd be the one who got into trouble.

After a bad day at school, I'll come home angry. Mom will tell me to do something like clean the cat litter, and I'll start yelling at her. I've held it in all day, so I just let it all out, and my mom is the one who gets it.

I wish the teachers would listen to us. I'd like to feel that they were listening.

SARAH

MOM WANTS US not to run away from our problems. She wants us to be strong and to feel good about ourselves. It's hard to feel that way all the time.

I get bullied a lot. Two girls ran up to me in the Breakfast Club at school one day and confronted me. They pushed me and called me fat.

Another time, I was on the playground and twenty or thirty kids all ganged up around me, laughing at me. I wanted to fight them all.

Eighth-grade boys started sexually harassing me, too, saying nasty things about my body—all sexual things. They even followed me home one day, laughing at me, making fun of me, and saying horrible things.

It even happens outside of school. I was sitting in the public library one day and saw that some kids were taking pictures of me with their cell phones. I told the librarian, and she got mad at them and made them leave the library. But they were waiting for me outside and I had to leave by another door.

It all started for me when I was in kindergarten. For some reason, the other kids got the idea that it would be funny to sit on me whenever I had to go to the bathroom. Like, five kids would sit on me and wouldn't let me go until I'd had an accident. Then they'd laugh at me for having an accident. That happened a lot.

I had a container of Jell-O thrown at me. It exploded on my shoulder and ruined my shirt. I've had kids call me names and tell me I couldn't play with them. Once, I head-butted a girl who made fun of me, and of course I got into trouble for that.

What happens is I'll come home all upset and I'll start ripping things up. It's like I get so mad that I need to destroy something or I'll blow up.

I would like to go to school and just learn and have fun without having to worry about all this other stuff. And I would like to know why these kids go after me. I'd like teachers to make us all sit down and listen to each other and hear both sides of a story.

WHAT DO YOU THINK?

• What do you think of Sarah's idea to have the teachers make them all sit down and listen to each other? What needs to happen next after that meeting?

• Does Patricia's anger make it easier or harder for her to deal with bullying?

In my old school a girl bullied this other girl by demanding money. She said the girl had to give her two hundred shillings every morning or get beat up until she fainted. The girl dropped out of school because she was too scared to go, and her future does not look good.

If you are bullied, report it to your prefects, teachers, and parents. If they don't stop it, go to the elders within the community. They will know what to do.

–JULIET NALULE,
TWELVE, UGANDA

MITCHELL, 16

I'VE BEEN BULLIED A LOT, starting in the sixth grade. I've also been the bully.

I started out being bullied. Those were hard days, going to school every day and not knowing what I was going to have to face. I'd get made fun of a lot, by older kids, by kids my age. They laughed at the way I looked, at the way I moved, at my size. I never said anything to the teacher. I didn't want to be a rat.

Going through that made me feel like crap, like I didn't want to go to school, that there was nothing good at school for me. Every day it would happen, at recess, in the classroom, in the hallways.

It affected my grades because I couldn't concentrate so well—I was too busy trying to protect myself and watch out for dangers. It affected the way I saw myself, the way I saw my teachers, and how I treated my parents.

In the classroom, kids would make rude comments—things the teacher couldn't hear. We'd go out for recess and I'd be pushed around. I was bigger than the other kids, taller and heavier, but that didn't stop them. They used that as a reason, because I was different.

At the beginning, I used to just take it. Then one day I just sort of snapped and started to fight back. All the name-calling, all the bad feelings—I'd just had enough. It happened on the playground, nothing special, just ordinary pushing and punching. But something snapped in me and I started to fight back. One kid pushed me and I went backwards, then another kid pushed me from behind, and in the midst of that my fist came out and I hit the ground.

That was the first suspension I ever got. We all got suspended for one day, all of us who were in the fight.

After you've been in a fight, you feel empowered; you feel like the Tough Guy on Campus. Before that, I'd always try to make myself smaller—kids laughed at me for my size, so I tried to hunch over. But after the fight, I realized that being bigger had its advantages.

The other kids didn't seem to mind that I'd stood up for myself. I think they even respected me a little for it. It took a while longer for my parents to notice the change.

But for the rest of grade six, kids left me alone. They stopped shoving me and calling me names. So fighting worked.

I got into a lot of fights in the seventh grade. It was a new school and I didn't get along with all the kids because I was different. The school I went to before only went up to grade six, so I had to switch to another school for grade seven and eight.

The way I dressed was one of the things different about me. I discovered punk music, especially the Sex Pistols, so I started to dress punk, which made me stand out. I got taunted a lot for that. One kid especially kept on me, so I let him have it. He was a bigger kid. That's always been the way. I always go after the bigger kids. I don't go after smaller people. There's no pride in that.

I got a three-day suspension for that fight. The kid who was mocking me had a reputation as a jerk, so a lot of kids thought he had it coming to him. Later on he got busted for possession of drugs, in the same school. I haven't seen him since then. He had to leave the school.

This fight happened toward the end of grade seven. I think I was able to keep from fighting so long, even when they were taunting me, because I knew they didn't know me. They were just taunting the outside of me, so I was able to not take it personally. They didn't know that I'm a nice person, really.

What changed at the end was that I got tired of taking it. By the end of the year, the guy should have known me, but he kept on treating me as if I was nothing. I'd had enough.

That was my only fight in the seventh grade, I think—because I lost! I didn't get badly hurt, but I did get roughed up a little.

In grade eight, there was less taunting, but I still got into fights. I was more popular then. Some kid in my class called me "faggy," so I got up out of my seat. I grabbed him from behind and swung him out of his chair. We fought right in the classroom while the teacher was out of the room. The teacher never found out, so I didn't get into trouble for that one.

I'm not sure why I picked that time and that kid to fight. I guess I didn't want other kids thinking they could call me names and get away with it. I needed to show them that I would stick up for myself. I was probably showing off a bit, too, because I was more popular then and I wanted to keep being popular.

There was another kid I went after in grade eight. We had a sink in the classroom, and I stuck his head in the sink and turned the water on. He was the kind of kid others picked on. I thought he was disrespecting me, and I wasn't going to take that from him. My friends congratulated me for going after him. His friends kept away.

Grade nine, I got into drugs. I went into high school thinking it was a fresh start. The teachers were all strangers. They didn't know I had a reputation for fighting.

The fresh start lasted about a week, and then I got busted for marijuana. I had to go through the courts, and then I got suspended from school for four days. After that, I stayed away from school as much as I could. I just went to my buddy's house and did drugs.

School seemed like a waste of time. I got through it by going to one class a day, then leaving.

Toward the end of the first semester, I quit doing drugs. I decided I'd better smarten up, so I went to school and managed to get all four credits. At the beginning of the next semester, I started doing drugs again—different kinds, marijuana, Ecstasy, coke. It's all easy to get, even in small towns. Even heroin. You just have to ask around.

I had a bad reputation with the teachers by that point, but I didn't really pay attention to that. I just got my credits for the semester and got out.

In the first semester of grade ten, I transferred to a high school in a different town, but I didn't go to class. My mom would drop me off and I'd get on my skateboard and just leave. This went on until December, then the school said, "That's enough. There's no way he's going to get his credits." So they made me leave.

I stayed around the house, and my friends would come over and we'd do drugs while my parents were out. Then my mother put her foot down and said she didn't want anybody over to the house when she or my father weren't there. So then I went over to my buddy's house. He was older, like thirty, and I was living there for a bit. My mother contacted Children's Services, and they put me into a foster home.

I agreed to go. Some days, I wish I hadn't, and

some days, I'm glad of it. But mostly I'm glad. I love it here, in this foster home. I'm going to miss it when I leave in a few months. I love the rules and the structure, and I love the people who are my foster parents. I feel safe here. And I'm getting all my credits this semester. I've stopped doing drugs. I've been handed a chance at a better life, and I'm not going to blow it.

I want to stay in school and get a good job when I'm older. I'm planning on becoming a video game designer.

If I hadn't been teased and bullied and taunted when I was a little kid, I don't think I'd be who I am. I think everything happens for a reason. If I hadn't had to go through that, I'd probably be part of the mainstream, not different. And I like to be different.

Having to be on the outside of things has been kind of a backhanded gift. All those years that I'd been bullied, some of it was pointless, but I've also been bullied for what I am. I'm bisexual, and that's really hard in a small town. Some people out here would like to shoot me for that.

I'm very open at school now about what I am. The people who are not my friends don't like it, and the people who are my friends don't mind.

Now, when I get called names, I just let it go by. I'm able to do that now because I know the truth about who I am, and I also know that people who

don't accept it have the choice to look the other way.

My parents know that I'm bisexual. I don't think they're approving of it, but they accept that's who I am.

There are some kids at my school who are just homophobic and look the other way when I walk down the hallway, kind of turning their backs. Other than that, nobody really says anything. They just see me as myself. I hope that's a sign that the world is maturing. And I'm not the only one at my school. There are lesbian and gay students who are open about who they are, so I'm not alone.

In my future, I see myself as a guy with a lot of imagination creating awesome video games. And I don't think I'll get into any more fights. I know who I am without having to do that.

WHAT DO YOU THINK?

- Do you think Mitchell's drug use was related to bullying? If not, why do you think he took drugs?

- Why do you think Mitchell feels safe in the foster home?

BETH, 15

I'M IN GRADE TEN. My mom works in the Bick's Pickle factory. They're processing hot peppers now. It's brutal work. The juice from the peppers makes her cough and sneeze, and makes her skin burn. She's very tired when she gets home.

I was bullied for two or three years when I was ten, then it stopped for a couple of years, around grade seven. Then I came to high school. In the first year of high school, there wasn't any bullying. Now there is.

It was my cousins who first started bullying me. I don't remember why. They'd chew up food and spit it at me. They made fun of my mom because she didn't have hair—she had cancer, and that made her bald. They'd call me names like "whore" and "slut." This would happen on the way to school and on the way home. They'd run after me and push and shove me. They'd knock me down. For no reason.

One time, my teacher was afraid of what might happen to me on the way home. He called my mother and asked her if it would be okay if he let me leave school fifteen minutes early. He thought I'd be safer that way. Mom said sure, but it didn't quite work. I move more slowly than other kids, and I was only halfway home when they caught up with me.

There have been a lot of problems at my school with kids other than my cousins. The kids were nasty, always whispering and saying things behind my back, just loud enough for me to hear them.

One of the teachers always put me down because I was slow in math. He'd tell me I'd never get it. He never gave me any encouragement. I'm not stupid. I just have a hard time with math and science. Reading and spelling, I'm good at. I even write poetry.

He bullied the other kids, too, yelling at them and grabbing some scrawny kid's shirt.

Mom got picked on really badly at school, too, so she understands what I'm going through. She hates school because of the bullying. When she goes into my school, it brings back all those memories. She says she gets anxious because she wants me to stay in school so that I can get a better job than she has. She wants me to go to college.

I'd like to be a musician and a singer, but I'm really shy of performing in front of other people. I'm afraid they'll bully me.

Sometimes teachers don't know how to handle girls. Like, me and my friends were always fighting. We'd get ourselves into these arguments, and even though we were miserable and tired of fighting, we didn't know how to get ourselves out of it. We needed help, and no one helped us behave better.

It got worse when a new girl came to our school. She really went after us. She called one of my friends "Seizure Girl" because my friend has epilepsy. She'd slam our fingers in doors, and she'd get us into trouble.

I'm in two remedial classes so I can get extra help with some things. I'm also in two credit classes and two regular classes. The teachers say if I do well in my remedial classes and don't get too stressed, I can move to all regular classes next year. I can take co-op, too, and work while I get credits. So it's pretty good.

The girl who bullies me the most is a year ahead of me, and she hangs out with all the tough girls in the smokers' pit. I used to sort of be friends with her. I even went drinking with her once, although I know I shouldn't have. But I was sick of being a good girl. Besides, she pressured me. But I'm never doing it again.

We stopped being friends after that, and now she bugs me. She says bad things about me to my other friends and tries to turn them against me. She's started threatening me, saying that she's going to kill me, she's going to get people to beat me up. She said, "They're going to smash your head open on the ground."

One day she says she's going to kill me. The next day, she says she's going to egg my house. Another day, she says I'd better watch my back because she's coming after me. It just goes on and on.

I was a wreck after she said those things to me. I kept looking over my shoulder. I couldn't sleep. I always had major headaches.

I told a teacher, and the police were brought in. The threats stopped for a while. But recently it started up again. She's calling me a rat, and giving me bad looks. She said, "Call the police if you want to—I'm not scared of them." So it goes on.

All the bullying I've had to deal with has made me stronger. I'm not going to just sit around and take it. I'm going to tell someone. I'm not being a rat. I'm just going to make sure I don't get hurt. Even if it doesn't hurt me physically, it can hurt me emotionally.

I struggle a lot with depression because of the bullying and lots of things, like worrying about my mom dealing with cancer. My mom and dad fight a lot, too, and that makes all of us depressed. We all have a rough time.

For a while I dealt with my depression by cutting myself. I felt so horrible—all these kids were calling me fat and stupid, and I started to believe them. The cutting was something to do. I don't do it anymore. I decided I needed a better way to deal with things, a happier way.

You need to learn to believe in yourself. You need to believe that you are worth a lot, and that you don't have to take the bullying.

Standing up to it is the best. Standing up makes you feel invincible.

WHAT DO YOU THINK?

- How does it complicate things when the bullying is being done by family members?

- Beth dealt with her depression by cutting herself. What other things could she have done that would have helped her instead of hurting her? What do you do when you feel sad?

AMANDA and SARA, 12 (twins); JULIA, 10—Sisters

JULIA

BULLYING STARTED for me in grade two because I was kind of new. We moved, and some kids were not very nice to me. Some kids talked behind my back, and some kids wouldn't include me. They'd make up all these clubs and talk about them in front of me, then say that I couldn't join.

It made me feel sad and excluded. At least my friends and I stayed together and stood up for each other.

The girls who excluded me at first came around eventually. They came over to me and we all played together.

So that was all fine for a while. Then we got older and things became difficult again.

Guys started teasing me. Kids would play truth or dare, and when I didn't want to do what they dared me to do, they'd make fun of me. But some of the things they dared me to do were just stupid. Like, they'd tell me to go sit in the middle of the soccer field when the older guys were playing so that I'd get hit in the head with a ball. That's just dumb.

So I made the choice that I didn't want to play with them anymore. They let me go because they could see that I didn't care about what they thought.

As I got older, I realized I had to make that decision about who I was going to hang out with. My parents could help me with the decision, but really, I had to decide. I want to be with kids who will make me do better things, not stupid things.

Sometimes I don't like what they say about me, and it hurts. But most of the time, they can say what they want. I know what's true.

AMANDA

BULLYING STARTED for my sister and me in grade six. Some girls had already started developing, and we hadn't started yet, so they made fun of us for not wearing bras. They'd laugh at me in the change room. My friends would stand up for me. I'm lucky to have good friends, but the teasing still hurt.

When I'd sit off by myself to read or to be with my own thoughts, kids would throw basketballs at my head. Then I'd move away or walk away, and they'd follow me and keep doing it. Or they'd chase me and tackle me. It just kind of made me feel like, *Well, what did I do that made you want to hurt me?*

I'm in grade seven now, and it still happens sometimes. But I try to keep my good friends close to me, the ones who judge me for who I am inside.

Before grade six, this wasn't a problem. In grade five, nobody had developed. Nobody had a bra, so it wasn't an issue. In grade six, everyone could see how some girls were developing faster than others, faster than me. I used to wish that I was developing like them, but over the summer I realized that I can't

change who I am. I can only accept who I am.

The boys didn't start bullying me until grade six. I didn't understand what they were doing at first—if they were just joking, or if they were trying to hurt me. Then they'd kick me and hit me and say I was ugly.

They picked on my friend, too. They called her ugly and other names.

I told the teacher and the principal, and they said they'd deal with it, but they didn't really deal with it.

My friend said she talked to the principal, too, but nothing changed.

Those kids aren't in my class this year, so they don't bother me as much now. They're going after other kids.

All this stuff happening made me feel really sad for a long time, but over the summer, I just realized that I am who I am, and I'm happy with that.

I made up a quote: "Life is like a storybook. People judge by the cover, but true friends look inside and read."

I learned that we shouldn't let people judge us or believe them when they do. Just decide how you think of yourself. Do you think you're beautiful? And I'd say, yes, I'm strong, brave, and beautiful.

When the guys were throwing basketballs at my head and following me around, I never turned around and asked them why. They were the bigger guys in the school, and I was scared of what they might do. I didn't want to deal with them. I just wanted them to go away.

If that were to happen today, I think I'd be able to ask them why they were doing it, because I know there's really no reason for it. I didn't do anything to them. I'm stronger now than I used to be.

SARA

FOR ME, BULLYING happened in grade five and six, because there were popular kids and unpopular kids. I was one of the unpopular kids, and the others would shut me out of their groups. I'd try to hang out with them and start a conversation, but they'd just ignore me.

Some people get upset with me. They think I'm just cute and little and that I get away with everything. They think I'm just a little kid because I'm short. I'm quiet and shy, too, so they think I'll never get into trouble. So they don't want to hang out with me.

I had a good friend who stood by me all this time. She said it didn't matter that we weren't popular, that we didn't have all the cool clothes.

The cool kids always looked like they were having more fun. They'd go places together and tell secrets to each other. They made you want to be a part of their group, and then it would hurt when they kept you out.

I'm in a different class now. The girls include me now.

Girls are really good at pushing other people out. I call it "the label game." They'll put labels on people without getting to know them, decide that's who they are, and treat them in a certain way because of that. I don't think that's fair.

There was a boy in our school who was bullied. He was called fat and ugly and he held his emotions in. The bullying got so bad that he eventually had to leave the school. The teacher told us about it after he left. I was so surprised. I didn't know it was going on. He was so nice all the time, but the bullying took place in secret—or at least away from us—and it really hurt him.

Our teacher was disappointed in us. She said this boy wanted so badly to be accepted. He even stole stuff from the school so that kids would think he was cool.

It's sad that you have to be bad to be accepted.

There's another kid in our class who has a minder with him all the time because he can't control his temper. Like, if his pencil breaks, he'll throw it. Some kids like to watch him lose it, so they'll quietly bug him and bug him until he'll scream and have a meltdown.

Our teacher has explained to everyone that this kid has some extra difficulties and challenges, but that hasn't stopped some kids from bugging him. It is hard to be in a classroom with him because he interrupts things a lot, but when kids bug him, that doesn't make it any easier.

I think teachers should pay more attention to bullying and do something about it whenever it's going on. And teach the kids who do the bullying what it feels like.

They keep on doing these bullying programs and repeating them every year, like bullying skits. But it doesn't work. Kids will say, "Oh, it's just a play, it's just a speech." But some of them don't really know how it feels to be bullied or to be a bully, so it doesn't really mean anything to them.

JULIA

KIDS NEED TO TALK to other kids about bullying. It's hard to talk to an adult about it because they don't really know our world. It's easier to talk to another kid about it. At our school, we have kids who go around in the building and wear special vests. They're called Peer Mediators. Kids can go to them and tell them things they don't want to tell adults.

AMANDA

KIDS WHO ARE being bullied need to feel that they are not alone, and kids who are doing the bullying need to know that they still have value, and they don't need to hurt others to feel important.

WHAT DO YOU THINK?

- Are there kids at your school who consider themselves to be the Cool Kids? Where do ideas about what is cool come from?

- Is there a program at your school where older kids are trained to help out younger kids? If so, does it work? If you don't have one, do you think it would work at your school?

KIRK, 16

IN GRADE SIX we moved to a neighborhood where there were a lot of high-class European-type kids, and my family was lower class and I was mixed heritage. So I didn't fit in. I got it every day. This was in grade six, seven, and eight—when I was twelve to fourteen. Before that, we were living in a mixed neighborhood, where people were used to differences, so it was easier.

But my mom wanted us in better schools, so we moved so I could go to a good school. She thought it would be a better environment—that rich, white kids wouldn't be getting into trouble.

Right from the beginning, these kids excluded me from games and teams. They called me names, racist names. Sometimes the teachers would overhear and they'd talk to the kids. The kids would stop for a few days, then start it up again. There were no suspensions, no consequences.

Once it went beyond just verbal bullying. Two of the kids came after me. I had to defend myself, so I punched one in the face and his lip busted open. The other one got scared and ran away. They both stopped picking on me after that.

I had grown a lot by then, and I was bigger than the boys who came after me. One kid's mom wanted me suspended, but it hadn't happened on school grounds. The kids were following me home—threatening me, calling me names. I hit them off school property.

The other kid's dad came over and talked to my mom. I think he understood that his son was a jerk because he said he didn't want me to be in trouble.

I'd told my mom what was going on with these kids. She said to just ignore it, but that didn't help.

There was one other mixed-race kid in the school, a girl. But she looked more European, so no one bothered her. And she kept away when they were bothering me. I can understand that. They would have turned on her.

I hated school at this time. My grades dropped way down. I felt bad about myself, and I hated it.

It wasn't until grade eight that I had friends who would stand with me, and that didn't happen until I split the lip of that racist kid. I know you're not supposed to fight, but nothing changed until I slugged him. After that, all the bullying stopped. For a while, everyone just kept away, then a few of them started being friendly. By the time we were ready for high school, all these kids wanted to be my friends.

I liked that, but it was confusing, too, because none of these kids had liked me in middle school. I asked them about it. A few of them actually apologized. Others said they were just being stupid because they were young. That was more of an excuse than an explanation, and it certainly wasn't an apology. But I don't hold a grudge.

After that, things at school were fine, even when I got to high school. I suppose I could have turned into the sort of guy who bullies others. I'm a big guy, and lots of kids who have been bullied become bullies themselves. But I remember what it felt like.

I don't have that state of mind to go after people. And I know my mom has high expectations for me. I don't want to let her down. (My dad's out of the picture. I haven't seen him since I was little, and I don't even miss him.)

I've turned into the kind of person that gets accepted by all sorts of groups. In my high school there are a lot of different groups: the preppy guys, the jocks, the hippies, the hard-core rocker kids, the skaters, the Goths—so many groups. And they all like me and accept me. I like that I can go from one group to another and just be myself.

I'm thinking of going into culinary arts. I love sports, too, and I love to read, mostly about history.

Going through all this has made me closer to my family. I was all alone at school. It took so much courage just to get out of bed and put my shoes on when it was a school day. I was always telling my mom that I was sick, but it never worked! It all made me think of the struggles my mom has gone through, and it made me respect her more.

I think it's better to be a nice person. They say nice guys finish last, but I'd rather finish last than have people afraid of me. I'd rather see people smiling than shaking.

WHAT DO YOU THINK?

- How do you react when you hear a joke that is made at the expense of someone of another race (or size or religion)? How do you react when the person telling such a joke is an adult?

- Do you think it's sometimes necessary to fight back once in order to stop some bullies?

Standing up for those who are bullied is a huge thing, but they also have to stand up for themselves. Some kids get bullied because they can't stand up for themselves. It's more important for them to change. I just think they need a little help to do so.

—SAE MORIOKA,
GRADE TWELVE, JAPAN

Talking About
YOU'RE TOO DIFFERENT

In this section, we have heard from kids whose differences—perceived or real—gave others an excuse to bully them.

• How many different groups are in your school?

• How difficult is it for kids to get to know other kids from different groups?

• Is there a difference between the way boys and girls react to kids who are not enough like them?

• How can we move beyond seeing differences to seeing what we all have in common?

• What will you take from your life now into your life in the future? What would you like to leave behind?

• What can you do if you think your teacher doesn't like you?

• Do you know any teachers who bully their students? What do they do? What power do students have in that situation?

• Do you know any students who bully their teachers? What can other students do to make the situation better?

On the third day of school, a girl called Barbara bullied me. She wasn't taller than me, but she felt like she had more power than me because she had been at the school longer. She bullied me because I was new, didn't speak English very well, and didn't have the same opinion as she did about things. After a month, I stopped her by telling her that not everybody has the same opinion. I reminded her that she had a first day at the school, too.

–KOLOINA RASAMOELY,
GRADE FIVE, MADAGASCAR

PART THREE

YOU'RE IT—JUST BECAUSE

WHEN WE ARE BEING TREATED badly, we often try to find a reason behind it. We try to figure out what we've done to bring this bad behavior down on us. We think that if we can find that reason and correct it, the abuse will stop. This way of thinking helps us feel we have some control over the situation.

But the truth is that the person doing the bullying has reasons that have nothing to do with us.

Even some teachers and parents cling to this idea that the targets have somehow brought the bullying on themselves. But when we do that, aren't we really saying that the target *deserves* to be bullied, that it's their fault, rather than the fault of the person doing the bullying?

As we say in You're Too Different, bullying creates its own reasons. Bullying is the problem, not the behavior or appearance of the target.

MARIE, 15; CARA LYNN, 11; and CHARLIE, 12—Siblings

MARIE

I WENT ALL through elementary school being bullied. I got picked on all the time. There wasn't any reason for it. Some kids will attack others over any little thing they think is different, and if there's nothing about you that's different, then they'll make something up.

I've learned as I've gotten older that if you're being bullied, it's never about you. It's all about the person doing the bullying. They're dealing with their own garbage, and they're not dealing with it very well, so it comes out in ways that hurt other people. The kid being bullied is just in the way.

It's the same if you have a boyfriend who abuses you, hits you, or puts you down. He'll say, "You made me mad," or "If only you would change, I wouldn't have to hit you." But it's his own garbage. You could change everything about yourself to try to please him, and he'd still hit you. He'd make up new reasons.

But it took me a long time to learn that. When I was young, kids would laugh at me for wearing glasses, or because I was bigger, or wore my hair in a certain way, or whatever. They'd hit me and poke at me and keep me out of games. They made my life hell. I came home crying all the time. I'd tell the teachers and the principal, but they didn't seem to do anything, so I stopped telling them.

Kids are always told, if you have a problem, go to a teacher, go to an adult; but if you tell them and they don't do anything, where do you go? I'd have crying fits in the morning because I didn't want to go to school. Then I'd come home and stomp around. It was just awful.

As I've gotten older and understand more what's going on and why, I've let it roll off me better. Kids will still try to pick on me on the bus sometimes, but I'm like, "Are you still doing that? You're so pathetic."

I'm in high school now. I don't have to deal with the kids who used to come after me in elementary school. It's a real relief. But even though I'm stronger now, all the bullying has changed me. It's changed the way I see myself. I have to work at remaining strong. It doesn't come naturally, the way it should.

There's a lot of pressure on teachers to stop kids from bullying each other, but parents need to take some responsibility, too. Mom would go to the parents of the kids who bullied me, and those parents wouldn't believe her. So, parents, if someone comes to you and tells you that your son or daughter is treating someone else badly, believe them and do something about it.

The hard part for me now is seeing my younger brother and sister going through what I went through.

CHARLIE

AT MY OLD SCHOOL, the teachers had all these rules: kids couldn't play tag, they couldn't do this, they couldn't do that. It's hard for kids to sit at desks all day and take orders and not have any breathing space. Recess is supposed to be our break, but then they add all these rules. I think that's why some kids bully. They've got all this energy and they have to put it somewhere. They pick on smaller kids because they'd get into too much trouble if they went after the teachers.

I'm in a new school now and things are going better. In my last school, I had a reputation for getting into trouble. So whenever anything went wrong, the principal would assume it was me. I mean, the principal really didn't like me and she was using her power inappropriately. A teacher even told my mom that it's good she got me into a new school because the principal was out to get me.

I got in trouble for everything, for going on the snow hill, for things other kids did, for all kinds of things. We had a church service one day in the gym and there were these grade-eight kids sitting behind me. They kept kicking my chair, making me mad. So I turned around to tell them to quit it, and I got in trouble, not them. Another kid said I'd pushed him off the bleachers when I hadn't.

Kids know when a teacher doesn't like a kid, and they use that to bully him. So they knew it was easy to get me into trouble. I think it was like a game, to see how often I could get yelled at.

One day the principal just pushed me to the limit. She threatened to suspend me for a week for something I didn't do. I went alone into her office and wouldn't come out, and I locked the door so no one else could come in. They finally had to get someone to take the hinges off the door.

I got suspended for that, of course, and when I came back, kids started accusing me of pushing them, so that was another suspension. I got so tired of all the bullying one day that I packed up my backpack and just walked out of the school. I'd had enough.

Some teacher saw me leave the school and they

called the police. I wasn't able to get far when the police found me and brought me back to the school in a police car. That got me another suspension.

I'm not saying all teachers are bad. I'm doing well at my new school, and the teachers seem to listen to us and they don't just jump on me when something goes wrong. I'm not so angry all the time now. Teachers are people, and people hold grudges. But they also have all the power, so when a teacher doesn't like a student, it's really bad for everyone.

If I could change anything, I'd like to see teachers follow through. Sometimes they'll say something like, if there's any bullying that happens, this and this and this will be the result. But then they get busy and they forget, and some kid will start bullying and totally get away with it.

CARA LYNN

FOR ME, BULLYING is the worst on the bus. Some kids call me names and make fun of me. They think it's fun to make people cry and make them afraid. The bus driver likes these kids, so I can't go to him and report them. It wouldn't do any good.

School is hard, too. Kids made fun of me for carrying a Tweety Bird backpack. We don't have a lot of extra money, so we can't afford to buy a lot of new backpacks. I told a teacher that kids were making fun of me, and she said it was my own fault for having a Tweety Bird backpack.

Kids will make fun of me for what I'm wearing, for shallow things. If we all wore school uniforms, then they couldn't make fun of my clothes.

My older sister, Shannon, used to be a peer mentor in grade six. I don't think they have them anymore, but it sounds like it was a good thing. They were kids that other kids could trust. If there was a problem on the playground, you could go to a peer mentor to help you out, instead of going to a teacher, who might be busy or have too much on her mind. A peer mentor would be interested in solving the problem, not in getting someone in trouble.

WHAT DO YOU THINK?

- Do you agree with Charlie that some kids bully because they have no other outlet for their pent-up energy? What would be a better outlet?

- What can you do when you're feeling really angry and no one will listen to you?

BARRETT, 16

I GREW UP IN a small town, and I've had a lot of experiences with bullying, starting in grade five and continuing even to today. Kids started teasing me then. I don't really know what it was—they were all my friends, and then one day they decided they just weren't.

I don't remember their words from back then, just that kids who were my friends all of a sudden were not. I don't know what happened.

I tried not to care. I tried to get some new friends, and they stuck for a while, then they stopped liking me, too.

I never asked them why. That would have been way too difficult.

When my friends started turning on me and dropping away, I talked to my mom about it. She apparently had the same problem when she was a kid. She never understood it either, so she had no advice for me. It's kind of weird that it runs in our family.

It made me into more of a keep-to-myself sort of person. I started just doing things on my own—things most guys don't think of doing. Like, I'm really good at origami, the Japanese art of folding paper into animals and things. It's a very exacting thing to do, to get all the folds right. The kids at school would see me doing this and it made me look weirder in their eyes. Anybody doing anything different, you're going to be made fun of. But that didn't make me stop. I ended up just doing more of it.

Maybe I felt like I had something to prove to myself, that I wasn't someone who would bow down to other people's ignorance. And part of me thought that if I could get really expert at it, people would admire me for it instead of laughing at me. Adults say they like it, but adults lie a lot. Kids will tell you the truth as they see it.

I never went to the teachers when I was teased. I don't recall teachers ever stepping in when kids got bullied, except to make it worse. So I didn't see how they could help me.

I witnessed a lot of fights at school, kids getting beat up. Some kids got really hurt. Teachers would break up the fights if they saw them, but often they didn't know what was going on.

I find, though, that the more rules there are, the worse the bullying gets. I'm in a school now where there are many rules and always supervision, always someone watching. Kids will try to go after other kids as a roundabout way of getting back at the staff, because they have to have some breathing room.

So I'm still a loner. I keep to myself and keep to my own interests. Soon I'll be an adult and will be able to shape my own life. I'm just waiting until then. I'm planning on going into fine woodworking as a craftsman.

Through all this, I've learned to use the strength that I have. I've learned a couple of new skills that will help me make my way in life, like patience and focus on detail, and the ability to be alone. All the people who are bullying me think they're hurting me, but really they are making me a stronger, better person. I know from them what not to be like, and I don't need just anybody to be with.

When I make friends in the future, it will be with people I respect and who respect me. Until then, I am happy to be alone.

WHAT DO YOU THINK?

- Has Barrett's focus on origami made thinks easier for him or harder?

- Do you think it's true that the more rules and supervision there are, the more bullying there is? If so, why do you think this happens?

At my previous school, my friend was being bullied. When we were playing tag everyone targeted him to make him "it." Whenever we had to pair up he was alone. I felt sorry for him but I didn't help him because nobody else helped him. I regret now that I didn't help him.

-KEI TAMAKI,
GRADE FOUR, JAPAN

COLTON, 10

LAST YEAR I was bullied a lot. This one kid—I won't mention his name—bullied me all last year. He called me names like "stupid" and other names. He called my friend names, too. I wasn't the only one he went after.

I'd gone to school with him since kindergarten, and he'd always been fine with me until last year. That's when he started picking on almost everyone. Most of it was aimed at my friend and me. He made us feel like we never wanted to come to school again. If we made a mistake on our work and he found out about it, he'd make a big deal out of it, laughing and saying how dumb we were. He called me an idiot and said "shut up" to me a lot, even if I wasn't talking to him. If he was around and I was talking, he'd tell me to shut up, as if he couldn't stand hearing my voice.

He messed up in school more than I did, but still he laughed at me and my friend. My friend was new, and I was kind of small, so maybe that's why he picked on us the most. Plus, I'm kind of sensitive, and some kids know whose feelings they can hurt easily. My older sister has Down syndrome, so that also makes me a bit different. But I'm not stupid and no one should call me that.

I told my teacher and he talked to this kid. This kid was bullying lots of other kids, so my teacher already knew it was a problem. This kid was angry all the time, like, out of control. So my teacher dealt with him but it didn't really do any good.

I didn't tell my parents about all the bullying until November, but it had started in September, right in the beginning of the year. I didn't want to go to school anymore. Sunday nights were terrible because I knew the next day I'd have to start a whole new week of being bullied by this kid.

A lot of things happened all at once in November. My great-grandmother died. I loved her a lot and I still miss her. A week after she died, our family dog died. He was fifteen years old, older than me. It was a lot to lose in one week. The bullying was one more awful thing to deal with it.

I started having nightmares about losing my family and about being chased and hurt. I hated sleeping in my room. I felt safer sleeping on the sofa, where I knew my parents were closer and could protect me.

So I finally broke down and told my parents about what was happening at school. I didn't tell them before because I wanted it to just go away, and I also wanted to handle it on my own.

My mom and dad went to the school a few times to talk to the vice principal and the principal. They were sort of supportive, but they never called it bullying. They have a zero tolerance for bullying, but it happens. And when it happens, they don't call it bullying so they can say that bullying doesn't happen.

I'm usually a really good student, lots of As and Bs on my report card. The only trouble I get into sometimes is for talking too much because I have a lot to say. But I don't want to go after other kids. I don't want to be someone who pushes or hits or insults other kids. Even if someone is calling me names, I don't want to be the sort of person who calls them names back. It isn't right to do that, and it doesn't help anyway. Kids who bully other kids are probably unhappy about something, so if I call them names back, they'll be even more unhappy and mad, and nothing will be fixed.

This bullying went on until the last week of school. During that last week, maybe the teacher gave this kid a really serious talking-to. I don't know. But for the last week of school, he left me alone. He ignored me. I was still afraid that he would say or do something to me, but he didn't.

But the whole school year up until then, I had to deal with it. The reason that I'm not dealing with it this year is because he's no longer in my class.

The theme at the school this year was the Peace Train, and every month we had an assembly about respect, and about being kind and not bullying. The whole year was an anti-bullying year. But this bullying is still going on.

My parents had a conference at school about me, and my mom got mad because she felt they weren't listening to her. They wouldn't listen to her when she told them I was being bullied, and she came home upset and frustrated. My dad does the school meetings now. He makes people listen to him.

It was a really hard year last year. I felt worried all the time that whatever I said or did would end up with this kid laughing and calling me names. And he shoved me one day, right into the mud. He shoved me from behind. All of it made the year hard. I couldn't relax because he was always around.

After I got shoved, my mom told my teacher to keep this kid away from me. The teacher said she would, but she couldn't be everywhere.

The anti-bullying assemblies we went to didn't

work on the kid who was bullying me, but they did start some good discussions among other kids, so I guess they were useful for that. I don't know what would have worked on this kid. He was too angry and too unhappy to be fixed by an assembly.

I don't know if it would have stopped him if I'd retaliated, like, if I had punched him or knocked him down. It doesn't matter. I didn't do that and I never would. I just didn't see how that would fix anything.

I was very lucky while the bullying was going on because I had friends who would stand with me. We'd all try to stand up to him together, so I didn't feel alone. When some kids are bullied, everyone stays away; the bullied kids must feel very afraid and lonely.

When the bullying happened, I started feeling really bad about myself. I started believing the terrible things that were being said about me.

But since the bullying has stopped, I've gained my self-confidence back. There are a lot of things I do well and enjoy, like art and building things. And I'm good at drama and music. So if you're a kid who's being bullied and put down, remember all the great things you have about you. The person bullying you doesn't know you. You know you, and you know how great you are. Remind yourself of that, and it will help you feel better.

WHAT DO YOU THINK?

- What do you think would make someone like Colton's classmate so angry they'd start to pick on a lot of kids?

- Colton says the anti-bullying assemblies at least got kids talking about it. Are there programs at your school that are more effective?

DENNIS, 12

I'M IN GRADE SIX. The bullies usually focus on kids who are smaller than they are, but they target just about anybody they want.

It was worse last year, but then one of the gang moved to a different country. The others don't bully as much without him, but it still goes on. Lots of name-calling, throwing things, intimidating—trying to make kids feel bad.

I'm in a gifted program. Our school is partly for gifted kids and partly for kids with problems who need extra help. There are kids who bully in both groups. Some of the kids are in that school because they got caught with the wrong crowd or because they *are* the wrong crowd.

In class I feel safe. I do my work and it's good. We do interesting things like make robots.

I'm bullied most at recess, usually when the teachers aren't watching. I'm small, and I'm often a target.

I've known most of these kids since grade one. Up until grade five they were fine. We got along. Then in grade five, they started growing up and getting bigger. They started getting more aggressive.

I'm a bit of a sensitive person and I don't really like being called names. It made going to school really unpleasant.

I haven't said anything to the teachers because the kids haven't done anything that serious. When you get to grade six, you don't go to the teachers unless it's really serious, like you're getting hurt. We're supposed to be able to take care of things like name-calling and verbal bullying by ourselves.

I've been going to this enrichment program since grade four. We do harder challenges and have more fun. But the bullying takes away that fun.

I don't really tend to speak up much, especially when things aren't going well. I don't know how I can make it any better just by talking.

I tried confronting the kids bullying me, just once. But it didn't stop. They just laughed and kept doing it. Most of the other kids know this is going on, but they stay away from it. They don't want to step in to stop it because they are also afraid of being targets.

Sometimes the kids have even called my mother names! It makes me feel so angry and upset because I can't stop it. I go home and I work out with my weights to try to get my anger out, but I can still feel it building up inside me. I just want them to stop calling me names, but I don't know how to make them. There are times when I come home from school in a rage. My mom is afraid I'm going to lash out, and then I'd be in trouble. I just want them to stop.

My mom helps when she can. There was a kid in Youth Group who really went after me, with names and other types of bullying. It was very, very bad, this one time especially. Mom saw it when she picked me up. She called this boy's mother and we all sat down together. The other boy was so unhappy, and he blurted out that he went after me because I'm so smart. I guess he has some struggles in school. He thought he'd feel better if he could make me feel worse. Just because I'm smart, it doesn't mean my feelings can't get hurt.

Dad says I should punch someone out sometime. He says that would stop the bullying. I'd get in trouble, but at least I wouldn't get the strap. Teachers used to be able to hit kids, but they can't do that anymore.

The good part is that I have one friend who always sticks up for me. He speaks to the bullies with the kind of courage that I don't have. He told me he doesn't want to be a bystander.

I don't know if next year will be better or worse. As you get older, you find yourself doing things you don't really want to do. The bullies get more powerful because they're older, and if you don't feel as powerful, it's harder to walk your own path.

When I finally do become older, larger, and more powerful, I'm not going to have anything to do with bullying others. I'm not that kind of guy. I know the consequences of hurting people emotionally.

Kids who are going through this need someone to stick up for them. I have a friend and my family, and it's still really hard. It would be unimaginably hard if I didn't have them. I'd be all alone.

WHAT DO YOU THINK?

- Do you agree with Dennis's school that verbal bullying isn't serious enough to report?

- Do you think Dennis is better off waiting until he is bigger to deal with bullying?

I think that ignoring people who are being bullied is not a good thing to do. Talk with the person who is being bullied or try to get them to talk to someone else who can help. It is hard to help someone who is being bullied because everyone thinks they will be bullied, too. But if you don't do anything, the bullying won't stop. Bullying won't stop unless you take some action.

—RITA HONDA,
GRADE SIX, JAPAN

JOHN, 9

IT ALL STARTED IN GRADE ONE. Every day I would get hit or punched in the stomach. Every time I went to tell the teacher, the kids would run away. The teacher wouldn't catch them at it, so they wouldn't get into trouble.

The teacher always said that the kids would get sent to the principal's office, but that never seemed to happen. So, every single day for practically half the year, I was punched in the stomach.

When I'd come home, I'd forget about it and get busy doing other things. Then I'd be back at school and it would happen again, and I'd remind myself to tell my mom and dad. But I didn't. I thought I could handle it myself.

The bullying kept on happening. I finally came home one day and decided to tell my parents.

The teachers never caught the kids in the act of hurting me, so that's why the kids didn't get into trouble.

But one day, the teachers did catch them, and that was the end of it! They stopped bullying me, although they went on bullying some other kids.

When I see other kids being bullied, I always run and tell the teacher. I know what it feels like; I know it's not any fun. I don't want other kids to be bullied.

Mostly now, the bullies leave me alone. Once in a while, they'll come after me. I guess sometimes they just need someone to bully, and if I'm around, they'll pick on me. They are one grade older than me.

There was another kid who bullied me. He was also a year ahead of me, and he'd bully, push, and hit me. Then we ended up in the same class. We got to know each other, and we became friends. Now we're best friends.

I asked him one time, "Why did you bully me?" He said he never did. So he never said in words why he did it, but he stands up for me now, so he shows it in his actions. I'm pretty thankful for that.

I loved going to kindergarten, but when it came to grade one, I'd cry every morning before getting on the bus. The bus driver asked my parents if I was getting picked on at school. When my parents asked me, I said no because I thought it would just stop.

Mom decided I didn't want to go to school because my teacher that year was really scary. She yelled all the time—the teacher, I mean, not my mom—and a lot of kids were afraid of her. I think that even my mom was afraid of her.

When I finally told my mom and dad what was going on, my mom called the school, and the principal said she'd keep an eye out for it.

The kid who was bullying me would wait until we were all going out for recess. He'd wait until I was sitting in the hall putting my shoes on, and that's when he'd attack me with a kick in the stomach or a whack on the head. It was every day, and it was so awful.

And then, when it was over, I was just so thankful.

I even said to the kid one day, "Okay, I get it, you're tougher than me, you've made your point. You don't need to keep kicking me. I get it."

I don't know what made me say that just then. I guess I'd had enough.

I think the guy's parents were fighting a lot, and he was unhappy all the time, and took it out on me because he didn't really know me. I wasn't anybody important to him, so it didn't matter. I can understand that. Sometimes I get just so darn stinking mad that I can't help it. I just want to give somebody a push or something. Just a little push.

The kid who used to pick on me is my good friend now. We stand up for each other against other bullies. There's one kid in our class who hits and punches and will even slam you with his back sometimes. Our desks are arranged in groups, and this kid sits close to my friend and will sometimes go after him. So I'm like, okay, this is not going to be a happy ending, but I'm going to try to stop it. You have to stand up for your friends.

We have two or three bully presentations every year at our school, and I enjoy them. They're funny, but they also teach. Sometimes, when we have recess or lunch right after a bully assembly, kids will start bullying each other worse than ever—like the assembly gave them some ideas. It's ridiculous.

To make my school better, it would help if there were more teachers watching the play area. We have one teacher at a time on the playground. They take turns, and they're all very good at watching, but they don't step in. They'll see this and that happening, but they won't stop it.

Now, if someone comes to them and tells them what's happening, they'll do something. But a lot of them just stand and watch. Older kids help out, too, on the playground. The older kids have a separate recess from us, so we won't get picked on by the bigger kids. A few older kids help out at our recess, and they do a good job.

I feel much safer at school now. Still, every morning I have some butterflies in my stomach because I don't know what will happen. I was scared for such a long time. I still remember what it was like.

From all this, I learned that it's not good to bully. Later on, you'll regret it. You might get a detention, and you might feel bad.

When I get older, I think I'd like to be a detective, or maybe a lawyer—somebody who stands up for people.

WHAT DO YOU THINK?

- One of the kids who bullied John became his friend. Do you think this happens often? How does this happen?

- Do you agree with John that more teachers in the schoolyard would make it safer?

MATT, 12

I'M IN GRADE EIGHT. I've lived in different towns all over this area.

Bullying has been a part of my life for quite a while. People have been pushing me, hitting me, and punching me for a long time.

There was a time when it didn't happen to me. I didn't know people could be so nasty to other people. It was just me and my friends, and we had fun.

My parents split up, and the moving began as they moved from house to house. I live in one town with my mom and stepdad, and in another town with my dad and stepmom.

I was first bullied in grade four. Some bigger kids

saw me as smaller and weak, and they didn't think I would fight back—but I do when I have to.

It surprised me when they started to act that way because I wasn't used to people behaving badly. At first I just let it go by. I didn't do anything.

Then I told my parents and the teachers and the bus driver, and none of that did any good. The kids kept bugging me.

So I started to hit back. I was like, "Screw this. If they're going to hit me, I'm going to hit them back."

Most of this happened on the bus.

There was one guy, the guy I usually sat beside. I wasn't doing anything, just sitting there, and he started kicking me and punching me. I told him to stop a few times but he didn't stop. So I hit him a few times. I gave him a massive black eye and a big bruise on his face.

After that, I transferred buses.

The kid who hit me goes to a different school. I only knew him from the bus.

Lots of things happen on the bus. Kids will take lighters and heat up the plastic on the seat to make it soft, then they'll stick the end of the lighter into the seat, to leave their mark. Some kids throw stuff—I got hit by a paintball pellet once. They throw all kinds of stuff.

Now I live so close to the school I don't have to take the bus anymore.

When I hit back at the kid who was hitting me, I was the one who got into trouble. The other kid lied and said I started it. I didn't have any marks on me because I blocked most of his shots. So they looked at me and they looked at him with his face messed up, and they blamed me.

I don't get bugged at school anymore. The last kid to bug me is now my friend. We used to be friends, and then his girlfriend dumped him. I went out with his girlfriend after that so he thought that we had planned this before, but we didn't. Now we've worked it out.

When he was mad at me, he bullied me a lot physically—pushing, hitting, kicking, choking. I had to go to the hospital once because of all the bruising and the choke marks around my neck. I'd hit back sometimes. Sometimes I'd tell the teachers. The teachers barely do anything. I'd get pushed right beside the teacher, and the teacher would quickly turn and look the other way.

I try not to bully people. I don't like being bullied, and I try not to bully others because I know how it feels.

I was really quiet at home when the bullying was going on. I'd either not talk at all, or I'd argue a lot. Mom was really afraid that I'd turn into a bully. I was so angry all the time. I had friends, but they didn't stand up for me. Maybe they were afraid. Maybe they didn't want to get involved in other people's problems.

It would have helped if the school had done something. The kid who was bullying me finally got suspended, but it took the police getting involved to make it happen.

I was the one who called the police. The bullying had been going on for a very long time. I was out on the playground, and this kid started hitting me again. I went into the principal's office and I said, "I've had enough. I'm calling my mom, and I'm calling the police."

I was just so sick of it. He had punched me one too many times.

The police believed me. I told the truth, and it sounded true, so they believed me. They talked to the other kid separately. I could hear the cop yelling, but I couldn't hear what he was saying, and I didn't really want to eavesdrop. They had me sitting in the little kids' library, so I just read all the kids' books to keep from hearing what was going on.

He was suspended for three days, but there were only three days left of school, so he got to leave for vacation three days early. What good did that do?

When you have kids who do drugs, suspending them is not going to stop them from doing it. They have to want to stop, and they need help to learn that they should want it. It's the same with people who bully. Suspending them does nothing. You have to educate them, make them go to a place where they can learn how to behave better. But still, they have to want to learn and change.

Anyway, he's my friend now. I don't really know how that happened. It's hard to explain. Friendship is kind of mysterious.

Mom doesn't feel good about me being friends with the kid who bullied me. She thinks he hasn't changed enough. But her best friend, a woman she's known for thirty years, used to beat her up in grade four. Now they're friends. So people can change.

They don't let us do anything at my school. They're afraid we'll get hurt. We used to play football with a rubber chicken. If you get smacked in the face with it, it doesn't hurt. But they stopped us playing that. Then we started playing hockey, but the teachers took our sticks away. They don't want us to have fun. We can't run on the pavement. We can't have bouncy balls because they might hurt the little kids. We used to have a separate little kids' section of the playground, but then the teachers said, "Little kids, run free!" and now we can't do anything in case a little kid gets hurt. We can't play soccer, we can't play British Bulldog. We play it anyway when the teachers aren't watching. I mean, we have to do something!

I know that I'm going to have to face another bully in my life. I'm only in grade eight. There's still high school and college to get through, and then there are bullies at people's jobs, too. Older people don't call it bullying. They call it abuse.

The experiences I've had with bullying so far will

help me fight back. And it's important to write everything down that happens and date it and sign it. Then there's a record, in case the police have to get involved.

Some people become bullies if they're sad, depressed, have family issues, or they've broken up with their girlfriend or boyfriend. Having some kind of problems sometimes turns people into bullies.

Also, there are some people who just enjoy seeing other people suffer, but I don't know why that is. It's not a normal thing. They have something wrong with their brains.

Teachers can help by actually listening and not worrying so much about stupid things like bouncy balls. It helps if the principal is strict, so people know what the rules are. Everybody likes things to be clear.

WHAT DO YOU THINK?

- Do you agree with Matt that children are over-protected at school? If so, why do you think this is? If you wanted to change that, what could you do?

- Do you agree with Matt that people who bully others have to want to change before they will stop?

One day, we met some students from another school, older boys who often bothered us. One of my friends threw a stone at them to get them to go away, but the stone hit one of the bigger boys on the head. My friends ran away. I stayed behind to say sorry, but I never got the chance because the bigger boys beat me. I started bleeding. A man chased them away and took me to the hospital. I was in a lot of pain and I almost died. I was out of school for a year. Now my mother has put me into a different school. If it weren't for bullying, I would be a year ahead in my studies. If that man had not helped me, I'd be dead.

Students, adults, and communities should be involved in the battle against bullying. Parents, you can help by becoming good examples to your children. Don't fight in front of us, we beg you!

–GILBERT BUSINGYE,
GRADE SEVEN, UGANDA

AMANDA, 12

I'M IN GRADE SEVEN. I'm good at math, French, and history. We're studying the Great Depression.

I have had a lot of experience with bullying. It's gone on for almost all of my school life. There have always been bullies bothering me. Some years were worse than others.

It started in kindergarten with name-calling. I thought then that this was just a normal way for kids to behave. Some days it would be easier and they wouldn't pick on me at all, and some days they'd pick on me a lot. It went on like that for the whole year.

It got worse as I moved on in school, even though I switched schools. Kids started following me around at recess. They'd poke at me and my brother Jonathan with sticks. We'd be so scared that my friend and my brother and I would stick right close to the teacher every recess. If we were right with her, the kids couldn't bother us.

There was one particular girl who was the chief bully. It started halfway through grade four. We moved here from another town, so I started midyear. Right off the hop, this girl started bullying me. She's the one in the class who most kids are afraid of. She's also the most popular girl because kids are afraid to get on her bad side. She's pretty, too, but as mean as can be.

She's even mean outside of school. I was down at Dollarama with my mom, my grandma, and my brothers. This girl and her friends and her father were outside the store. She started calling me swear words. She called my mother a fat pig. This was three years ago. She was screaming these terrible things right in front of the Dollarama! Right in front of her father! My mom wanted to say something, but I was too scared of what the girl would do in return, so I said, "Let's just get out of here." Since then, it's never stopped.

In grade five, I wasn't in her class, but there was another girl in my class who bothered me. There's a small group of them that make life miserable for everyone. In grade six, I was back in the first bully's class.

It's gotten worse and worse. Mom says it's made me difficult to live with because I take it and take it and take it at school, and then I come home and lash out at my family because I feel so bad. I tell my mom a lot of things, but there's also a lot I keep inside.

I've done what I'm supposed to do. I've gone to the teachers; I've gone to the principal. I've talked to counselors, and this kid still picks on me, so what's the sense of telling anybody, really?

This past spring, I was at the park with my family, and this girl was there, and she started screaming at us, swearing at us and calling me names and being really horrible. We were trying to ignore her and have a nice day at the park, but as soon as she showed up, it was over.

We went home and my mom called the police. They said that if this girl is in the park, then don't take your family to the park. But why should we be punished? We're going to the park to have fun together as a family, and she's going to the park to make people miserable. Why should she get to be there and we can't?

It settled down for a bit over the summer. Mom contacted the principal and told her that if there was even one more incident, one more name-calling, that she was calling the police again and would have the girl charged. Maybe the principal talked to this girl, because it stopped for a while.

It started up again at the end of August. She'd be outside the library and call me "Teeth" or "Buck-Teeth" or "Beaver Teeth." All that. Both my brother and I are scared that if Mom says anything to her, she'll just beat us up at school.

I didn't want to go back to school this fall. I wanted to change schools, but there was no room for me in the other schools.

That girl is not in my class this year, but her friends are. They started calling me names again. I told the teacher and the principal, and the teacher said, "Well, if you stop bugging them, they'll stop bugging you," but I'm not the one who is bothering anyone.

The principal said she's not going to do anything more because I've had so many problems with this before, she's starting to think it's me that's the problem. She says I'm old enough now to walk away and ignore it.

But if I come to the end of my patience and hit this girl to get her to leave me alone, I'll be the one who gets into trouble. Nothing will happen to her. She's tormented me for years and years and gotten away with it. But if I hit her, even just one time, I'll be in big trouble. It's not fair.

With the other girl, she and her friends would throw sticks at me and my brother. She'd have a huge group of kids with her, and they'd surround us and poke us with sticks. We'd stay by the teacher, but sometimes it would seem like the teacher was kind of impatient with us hanging around her—depending on the teacher. You can tell if a teacher doesn't really like you.

I have one friend at the school, but she doesn't stand up for me because she's afraid she'll start getting picked on, too. So really, it's just me against half the school.

I sometimes eat my lunch in the detention room, just to get away from them. They really tease me about my teeth. I can't eat my lunch in the lunch room because the kids will tell me, "Oh, take a bite of your sandwich," and then I will and they'll start cracking up laughing because of the way I eat. I don't eat any differently from the rest of them, but they're so dumb they'll make up things to laugh at.

A boy in my class the other day called me Beaver Teeth, and I just turned to him and said, "You know, the whole teeth thing is really getting old!" We're in grade seven now. It's time for everyone to grow up.

He looked surprised when I said it. Kids are used to me not saying anything. So it shut him up for a little while.

But it didn't stop. They pull my hair in class, poke me with rulers when we are doing projects. In gym when they're supposed to be practicing kick-passing, they'll kick it way out in the field when it's my turn and laugh at me when I have to run for it.

It will probably never stop.

My grades are really good. I get straight As. But sometimes I will slack a little, I admit, because I'm so worried about what recess will be like that I stop concentrating on my work. But when that happens, I always seem to find a way to pull my grades back up.

It really frustrates me when the school doesn't do anything. I went to the principal the other day about kids bullying me, and she was very short with me. When I left, I heard her sigh, a sort of I-wish-this-kid-would–stop-coming-to-me sigh. They probably do get tired of me going to them. One day I was in the office five times to complain about bullying. I can understand them being tired of it, but really, that's their job.

I don't feel safe going to school. I'm always worried about being attacked or insulted rather than focusing on important things. I worry about how I will avoid the bullies, and what they might do when they see me. There are nights when I can't sleep because I'm worried so much.

I take a risk every day because I have to go to school. I have to keep up with my schoolwork. Whatever happens happens, and I try to deal with it.

I would like the teachers and the principal to call in the police to talk with the bullies, so that they know it's serious. The really bad bullies have parents who don't care about them. They're allowed to do whatever they want. Some of them are roaming around the town at midnight by themselves. My mom and I see them when we go out to the store for something. They're hanging out by the church or skateboarding by the library. It's midnight and they're twelve years old, so clearly their parents don't care about them. They probably know their parents don't care, and that makes them angry inside. Then they take it out on people like me. If their parents started caring, maybe they'd leave me alone.

I don't think the bullying affects how I see myself because I don't care what they say about me. It affects how angry I get. I get angrier and angrier, and that affects how people look at me. They see me as a really bad person just because I'm getting angry over bullying. And a lot of people don't believe me when I tell them what's going on. Grown-ups expect us kids to just deal with things that they would never put up with. If they went to work every day and had people calling them names and poking them with sticks when they sat at their desk, they'd know that bullying is serious.

When I grow up I'd like to be a lawyer, the kind that stands up in court and tells the judge to put criminals in jail.

I've heard that things get better in high school. You have more freedom there and there are a lot more kids, so chances are good that at least some of them won't be jerks.

Meanwhile, I have two more years to get through. I love to write a lot, and if I work on my writing, that might help me to get through it. I love poetry, especially rhyming poetry, and I love writing song lyrics.

People do bad things when they think they can get away with it. If teachers were stricter, then kids would have to behave better.

WHAT DO YOU THINK?

- Is it possible for teachers and principals to get so used to seeing someone like Amanda bullied that they start to think it's her fault?

- What can you do when people behave like jerks in public places?

REBECCA, 19

WHEN I WAS SIXTEEN, someone started a really bad rumor about me, a rumor that is still going around. The rumor was that I had AIDS.

It was started by the girl who, up until that point, had been my best friend. We were at a party together and she flipped out on me. I later learned she'd been on cocaine that night. Cocaine sounds glamorous, but, believe me, it can make you really, really ugly.

We'd been friends since we were little. Our mothers grew up together, and we'd talked about our own daughters one day being friends, too. It was going to be this long, unbroken chain of friendship. But it all fell apart.

The cocaine made her flip out. She started beating me, hitting me for no reason that I can think of. It came out of nowhere.

She was pregnant at the time—how stupid is that, taking cocaine while you're pregnant!—and I remember thinking I had to be careful while I tried to push her off me. I didn't want to do anything that might hurt her baby.

I got away from her with just bruises and scratches, and right after that was when she started the rumor.

I don't know why she chose that as the rumor. We'd never discussed AIDS, it wasn't a topic of conversation with our friends. We learned about it at school, I guess, but I don't know why she chose that.

It affected my life in a huge way. It got so bad I didn't even go to school for a while. When I went, all day long kids would be questioning me or making fun of me. When I'd pass by kids in the corridor, they wouldn't say, "Hello, Rebecca," they'd say, "Hello, AIDS!"

It's so stupid. AIDS is a medical condition, like cancer or meningitis. The people who have AIDS are just people, no better or worse than anyone else. But the way kids reacted—it was just stupid. But it hurt. AIDS is serious. It's nothing to make jokes about.

I think it was especially bad because I was going to a Catholic school. AIDS is a disease that some gay people get, and the Catholic Church hates anything to do with gays.

Some kids wouldn't come near me. Some kids that I'd known for a long time wouldn't talk to me. Some kids, when I'd walk down the hallway, would flatten themselves up against the lockers to avoid coming into any contact with me. Totally stupid. Everyone knows you can't get AIDS just by touching someone, but these kids thought it was such a big joke to pretend I was poisonous or polluted. They wouldn't want to touch anything that I had touched.

I told my mom what was going on. She tried to support me and to help me, but there wasn't much she could do. It was a rumor. You can't hold onto a rumor and make it stop. It has a life of its own.

And I don't—and didn't—have AIDS, but it was hard to figure out how to protest what they were doing to me without making it seem like it would be okay to do it to someone who really did have AIDS. None of it was okay, and not just because it was not true.

It was horrible. I even went and got tested for AIDS, twice, just to prove to everybody that I didn't have it. But even then a lot of people didn't believe me.

The rumor spread beyond the walls of the school, out into the town. I used to work at McDonald's. I just got fired before Christmas, and I found out that the people I worked with were calling me "AIDS Girl" behind my back. This was just a month ago, and the rumor started three years ago. I don't know if that had anything to do with why I was fired or not. The reason they gave for firing me seemed pretty lame, but I'll never be able to know for sure. Before I was fired, people who had been nice at the beginning became very rude and weird around me, acting like the kids did at school. And I could tell when I turned around that they'd say stuff or make gestures about me, or I'd enter a room and they'd stop talking but stand there, smirking. People think their targets don't know what they're doing, but the targets know, and the people targeting them just come off as real asses.

This girl who'd started the rumor eventually came up to me and admitted starting it. She said she'd just decided I had AIDS—no particular reason—and she felt like telling everyone. I told her how the rumor had hurt me, but she said she didn't care, and just walked away.

My sister's best friend is gay. He used to get harassed really badly when he first came out, and at his work place, too. I talked to him about the rumor. He told me not to listen to it, that there are always idiots, and they weren't worth being upset about. It's hard to do, but at least I had his example to follow. All he went through—and he's still strong.

I hated going to school. Teachers became aware of the rumor and they'd stop me in the halls to ask me about it. I even got called down to the office and they questioned me about it. I told them exactly what was going on and that it was a rumor. They were really understanding, and they said if I needed anything to just ask. But something told me they didn't believe me. You know that feeling?

I switched schools and am now six months from graduating. Things have quieted down. I still get people coming up to me on the street, or calling out AIDS when I walk by, but much less than before. I think it will eventually just fade away.

I've been bullied a lot in my life, since grade four and five. I used to have no friends. I was bullied terribly, I think, because I have a learning disability and had to go to special classes. I have a non-verbal learning disorder and left-brain dysfunction. It affects my fine motor skills, like writing, and I have a hard time with math. It's gotten better. I've had a lot of help at school and it gets easier to deal with as you get older. You learn ways to work around it. But still, some kids will pick on any little differences, any little weakness, to make someone else feel bad. I'd go home crying almost every day.

But I did meet one of my best friends ever around that time—not the girl who started the rumor but another girl. This one stood by me all the time and has made everything easier.

My mom has been a big help, too. When I was younger and would come home from school crying, Mom would go to the school and yell at people; and things would get better for a while.

When I was really young there was another girl who always bullied me on the bus. She was horrible to me. One time she threatened to kill me, then she threw her open pudding cup at me, ruining my brand new shirt. I bawled. Mom was waiting for me as I got off the bus. Mom went onto the bus and demanded to know who had done that to me, and then she screamed at that girl—just screamed at her. She made that girl feel about an inch tall. After that, the girl left me alone. None of the other bus kids bothered me, either.

All these adults who say they can't do anything about bullying—they should take some lessons from my mom!

I've applied to college to become a deaf-blind intervener and personal support worker. I think I'll be good at it because I know what it's like to feel vulnerable. And if anyone ever tried to bully my students, I'd come after them; I've learned from my mom! They'd be in a lot of trouble, and they'd never do it a second time.

All the things that have happened to me—I've learned that I am above all that. You should never allow bullying to make you feel bad about yourself. Usually the bullies want to drag you down to their level. You have to remember that you are better than the bullying. Being bullied doesn't define who you are. Only you can do that.

WHAT DO YOU THINK?

- Do you agree with Rebecca that there isn't much that can be done to stop a rumor?

- Is there anything Rebecca's friends could have done to stop this rumor or at least lessen its impact?

HERMAN, 10

I LIVE IN A LITTLE house that used to be a place for storing asparagus.

Our family is Low German Mennonite. We lived in Kitchener for a long while, and everything was great there. I had lots of friends, and even people who weren't my friends treated me well.

Then we moved down here. I've been pushed around. I've had my lunch money stolen. I've been called names.

The boys who were doing this were much older. They were supposed to be in high school, but they had to come to my school for special lessons because they weren't ready for high school. Part of my school is a school for Mennonites who have just come up from Mexico. They come to our school to get used to Canadian schools and learn English. Most of the big kids leave us alone, but these two guys were angry about having to go to a special school, and they took it out on me.

It made me sad all the time, and angry. I was ashamed. I was afraid if I said something they'd just do it worse.

They'd bully other kids, too. They pick on some kids and leave others alone—they can smell fear. They bullied me the most because I was new.

They'd call me fat and ugly. They'd call me "Her" because that's how my name starts. It really hurt my feelings, and I stopped doing so well in school.

It was hard to keep my mind on my work because I felt so sad and scared. I didn't want to get out of bed on school days and I didn't want to leave the house.

One time, I faked being sick and my mom let me get away with it, but only once—and I think she knew I was faking.

I didn't tell anyone what was happening for a long time, but it showed that I was unhappy. I kept it together at school but by the time the day was through, I couldn't hold it in anymore. I'd yell at my sisters and slam things around. I'd even yell at my mother. I was angry all the time and there was no rest in my mind.

It made me so unhappy! I wasn't used to being treated so badly and I wasn't good at dealing with it.

I had a couple of friends, but they didn't stand by me when the bullying was going on. They were too afraid. I don't blame them. They're still my friends.

Whenever these big guys pushed me or called me names, I'd try to stand up for myself. I'd try. I'd tell them they weren't very nice and all they did was bully people who were smaller than them. The bullying didn't stop but at least they knew how I felt about it.

I think if they had only bullied me, I wouldn't have been able to say anything because I'd be too busy being scared. But I'd see them bullying other kids, too, and that made me braver. I had to speak out for all of us.

Finally I told my mom and dad, and they helped me. We went to the principal and the principal stopped it. And then I went to a place to learn new ways of dealing with my anger. They helped me learn how to deal better with bullies if I'm ever bothered again.

I'm a lot calmer now. My whole family is happier when I'm so calm.

It's a good thing to be calm. I want to be a truck driver like my father, and you have to be calm when you're driving a big truck.

WHAT DO YOU THINK?

• What would older boys get out of going after someone like Herman, who is so much smaller than they are?

• What would make the younger students at your school feel more comfortable around the older students?

I had a friend who was bullied in many ways that affected her physically and academically. She had to act as a maid to her perpetrators, giving them her food and pocket money. This made her lose focus in her studies. Finally, she reported it to someone who could help her.

−SHADIA NAGUJJA,
FIFTEEN, UGANDA

Talking About

YOU'RE IT—JUST BECAUSE

It's distressing to become the target, and it's natural to try to find some reason behind it so that we can make sense of our experience. But bullying doesn't need a reason. Bullying is about power—about someone trying to make themselves feel bigger and stronger by making someone else feel smaller and weaker.

• When someone is bullied over a long period of time, how long does it take before they feel safe again?

• Have you ever been the target of a rumor? Have you ever been part of spreading a rumor around?

• What's the difference between gossip and the harmless sharing of information about your friends? Is there a difference?

• What sort of bullying happens on the school bus? What would make things better?

• What are the consequences of bullying at your school? Are they effective? Why or why not? What would be more effective?

When I was in grade two, this new girl, Maya, brought a plastic racket for after school. Yoni, Feryl, and I hid it behind her shelf. When the bell rang to go to class, Maya couldn't find her racket and didn't know why it was lost. We went to class and Miss Nelly asked us where we put the racket. We had already done lots of bad things to Maya, so she knew it was us. We wanted to be honest, so we showed Miss Nelly where the racket was. After school, we had to write a letter to our parents about the incident. From that day on I decided I was not going to bully anyone again. I was scared about what would happen if I had to give my parents another letter. I didn't like their disappointment and anger.

—LINDA DIAMONDRA RAZANADRAINAIRISOA, GRADE FIVE, MADAGASCAR

PART FOUR

WE WANT TO CRUSH YOU

Sometimes bullies pursue their victims to a dangerous degree. Their behavior, unchecked, grows in strength and cruelty. The person who bullies feels that anything they do is acceptable, that the person they are bullying has no value. It doesn't matter if their victim disappears.

Those who bully to this extreme often have people around them who prefer to follow than to go their own way. The bullying almost takes on a life of its own as this group abandons its senses and morals and moves in for the attack.

"Bullycide" is a new word. It means bullying that results in the victim's suicide. We hear their names on the news and see their pictures in the papers, young people who were bullied so severely that it led to suicide or murder. When the news breaks, we ask ourselves how it could have happened. How could people treat other people so badly? How could the attackers think they could get away with it? Why didn't anybody stop them?

The children in this section talk about being relentlessly hunted and tormented by the people bullying them.

CHELSEA, 19

This happened to me at the end of grade eight.

We were all in the gym, taking down the decorations from our graduation party the night before. There was an easy feeling. It was the end of school, and we weren't being supervised.

Kids went in and out of the gym all day, and I learned later that they were putting together a Web page about how much they hated me.

There was one girl who started it. She created an Expage—this was before MySpace and Facebook. The title of the page was Let's Kid Redhead's Ass. Redhead meant me. She put everyone's name on the page and got them all to write down what they didn't like about me.

Everybody did it. Even kids who were my close friends. They said she told them it was just a joke, but they could see the other things that had been written, and they were not funny.

I didn't learn about it until the end of the day. Some kids told me about it after school was over. I came home and told my mom, and we looked at it together.

It was horrible. There were threats on the page, and insults. Really nasty things.

My mom printed out the page and took it to the school the next day. The teachers were still there even though classes were over. The school didn't know what to do, so they involved the police, but no charges were laid. It was the end of the school year, and I think everyone just wanted to be done with it.

I was devastated. I couldn't believe this bad thing had happened to me. These kids were the kids I had grown up with!

I didn't talk to anyone the entire summer. I felt like I didn't have any friends anymore. We live a little ways out in the country, and that made it easier for me to hide. If I didn't go into town, I wouldn't run into anyone I didn't want to see. Mostly, I stayed in my room. I stayed in bed. I didn't even leave the house most of the time. The whole summer was lost.

Mom tried to help by getting girls my age—daughters of people she knew—to come over, but that didn't work out too well. You can't arrange playdates for someone who's thirteen. But I love that she tried.

My grade-eight teacher knew this had happened but never called me to see how I was. My best friend apologized and her parents apologized. She said she'd thought it was just a joke, and she didn't write anything really bad—she just wrote something about my freckles, and she has more freckles than I do. It's something we've always kidded each other about. So it wasn't what she wrote that hurt, it was the fact that she participated with the others. It helped a lot that she apologized.

My friend Patrick also wrote something on the Web site, and afterward he wrote me a really nice letter to say he was sorry.

But generally I didn't hear from kids. I heard from parents. At one of my sisters' soccer games, a classmate's mom said to my mom, "My son is really sorry. He didn't mean what he wrote, and he is in a lot of trouble from us." He couldn't tell me himself at that time. I understand more now how it is with grade-eight boys. I appreciated that he apologized through his mother.

But some parents were very strange. Some called to deny their kid had anything to do with it. Some of them were angry at me, as if I had made myself into a target. And some were angry at my mom for making such a big deal out of it.

At the time, I didn't see any of this coming. Looking back, it's easier to see what led up to it.

My friends and I had gone to school together since kindergarten. We were a very close group. The girl who did the Web page about me came to our school in grade six, and she never really fit in. I was also a really good athlete in track. She was good, too, but never quite as good as me.

She never liked me, but she wanted my friends to be her friends. She hung out with our group, even came to a couple of my birthday parties. She hung around us, but she was never a part of our group. She was just different.

I can usually recognize when kids come from a difficult situation, but I couldn't tell with her. I never got close enough to find out. To tell you the truth, I was a little afraid of her. I'd never outright tease her. She seemed a little loud or unpredictable. And she dressed differently from the rest of us. We all wore Northern Getaway clothes and leggings and headbands, and she wore tight jeans and tops. I guess I just assumed she was jealous.

Then, too, at the graduation ceremony, there was a big fuss made over me. I was Female Athlete of the Year again, even though she almost beat me in the 100-meter race. I had to stand up on stage while our favorite teacher made a long speech about me and gave me an award. She probably hated that.

The day after that was when she set up the Web page.

We went to different high schools after grade eight, but I saw her again when we were in grade ten. She came into the drugstore where I worked. I couldn't be rude—I was working—but I wasn't any more helpful than I needed to be. I've never asked her why she did the Web page. I've never asked her for an apology.

Having this happen to me has definitely changed me. It's made me more aware of how people suffer.

Before this, I was just a bystander. Things would go on around me that I knew were wrong, and I'd just let them happen without saying anything.

For example, there was a kid we'd gone to school with for years who had a speech impediment. Kids were always picking on him. I didn't tease him, but I did nothing to stop it, either. Nobody did. One day in grade seven, he was being teased by some kid during class and he answered back. The kid who was teasing him stabbed him in the shoulder with a pencil crayon. The pencil crayon went right into his back. It stood right up in the muscles of his shoulder.

When I think about that now, I think that if I and others had stood up for him years earlier, then it would have been off-limits to tease him about the way he talked, and he never would have been stabbed.

This Web-thing happening to me was a wake-up call. It was meant to hurt me—and it did—but it also made me look at my life. I was on top and everybody liked me, and I took that for granted. I never had to consider other people's feelings. If this hadn't happened to me, I could easily have ended up as one of those shallow, gossipy, drama-loving girls who don't really contribute anything to the world.

So, I guess you could say she did me a favor.

WHAT DO YOU THINK?

- How do you think the girl who set up the hate Web page got so many kids to go along with her?

- Chelsea came out of this experience with a greater compassion for others. She could have come out of it wanting to hurt people. Why do you think she made the decision to go one way instead of the other?

CORY, 15

I AM IN GRADE NINE NOW. I've been bullied since grade two.

In kindergarten and grade one, I went to a school where everyone liked me and I liked everyone. Then, halfway through grade two we moved, and I had to switch schools. And that's when it started. Mostly then it was just name-calling and treating me as different because I was a new kid.

It got worse later on. It got really bad in grade six and seven, as the kids bullying me were older and stronger and better organized. Sometimes it would be a group, sometimes just a few kids. Sometimes one kid would start it off and others would join in, like a game. They'd do all sorts of things, like drag me along the ground, hit me, throw things at me. It would happen every couple of days—and if it wasn't happening, I'd be afraid that it would happen.

Most things happened on the playground. There were teachers around, and sometimes they just stood and watched without doing anything.

Last year, this group of guys came at me on the playground. They surrounded me and tried to grab me. They said they wanted to airplane me—you know, throw me through the air. I curled up in a fetal position to try to protect myself, and I was kicking out at them and yelling at them, but there were a lot of them. They grabbed me by my feet and swung me across the school yard. My whole back was cut up from skidding across the yard. They picked me up and just threw me.

The whole time this was happening, a teacher was close by, watching the whole thing. And the funny part was that she was a good friend of my mother's. So when Mom got out of me what had happened and saw the damage done to my back, she called the teacher up. The teacher said she thought we were all just fooling around. A group of kids, all of them twice as big as me, surrounding me, and I'm yelling and trying to get away—and she thought I was having fun? She just didn't want to deal with it.

Mom went to the principal a few times and it didn't help. One time, the principal called me into her office and made me go over every detail. She questioned me as though I was lying, as though she was a cop trying to get me to confess something.

Nothing happened to the kids who attacked me. Maybe she talked to them, but that's it. They bullied me worse afterward.

After the airplane incident, Mom called the police and asked if she could press charges against the kids who did that to me. The police said, yes, since it was clearly an assault. Mom was ready to do that, but instead she called the parents of the lead attacker. His parents made a show of not believing her, of not believing that their son could act that way, but he was much better after that, so they probably told him off. Maybe he just needed to be reminded that he was hurting someone who wasn't hurting him. He even stood up for me a couple of times when his friends started to go after me. We're not friends now, but at least he leaves me alone.

He told the other kids in his gang that Mom nearly called the police. Then they bullied me just to the edge of what's legal, to avoid getting into trouble.

I'm on the bus to and from high school every day with these guys. Usually, going to school in the morning is all right, because everyone is too sleepy and miserable to go after me. But the way home is different. They smoke a joint before they get on the bus, so it's fun for them to go after me. Already this fall I've been whipped with zip ties, those plastic ties with edges on them. My arms and neck were all bloody.

They've thrown my books out the window of a moving bus, and they've scrawled *Cory is an asshole* in the textbook that I'm supposed to return to the school in good condition at the end of term. They've thrown my backpack under the bus so that I have to crawl under to get it. And the bus driver does nothing. She jokes with the kids who are going after me.

Mom called the school when my arms got all ripped up, and the police officer was brought in to investigate it. The officer confirmed that the bus driver had witnessed the attack; and if that happens again, the boys will be charged.

It keeps going on, but they haven't drawn blood again.

I never know when an attack is going to happen. I'm not watching my back all the time. I'm trying to enjoy my day. But it's always in the back of my mind. I'm used to it.

It's taken away my confidence. I was a different kid when I first started getting bullied, before the serious stuff started to happen in grade six. It's affected my schoolwork a few times, but not often—I just got my report card today and I have an eighty-one percent average. I focus hard on my schoolwork so I don't have to think about the bullying. But it bums me out.

They gang up on me, I feel horrible about myself, then I bring it home and take it out on my family. And the whole house gets upset.

I used to be so assertive and so confident and so ambitious. I try to move on and leave it behind, but it's hard.

I don't want to be aggressive. I don't want to lash out at others. So when girls are punching me in the back of the head or slapping me in the face, or when smaller kids come after me because they see kids in my class doing it, I don't know how to respond. I won't fight back, and they see it as a sign of weakness.

But now I'm starting to change that approach. I'm getting ready to fight.

I'm very thin, like a reed, but I play football and I'm very strong.

There's one guy who is the biggest problem, but only when he's with his buddies. He'll punch me or whatever. When he's alone, he stays away from me, because he knows I'm strong. Mom says that now if I have to fight to defend myself, she'll back me up.

I'm in high school now, and while I'm at school, everything is fine. Kids like me, I like them, I like the school. It's just the guys on the bus ride home. All the kids who bother me do drugs, big time.

The grade nines and tens ride a different bus from the older kids. I've heard that the older kids' bus is even worse, with more drugs and more violence.

Stuff is ongoing. For example, I got eighty-nine

percent on a geography test. I told my mom, and she wanted to see it. One of the kids had got hold of it and written *Faggot* across it in big letters with a magic marker. I didn't want to show her that.

I don't sleep very well. My mother says I scream out in my sleep all the time. I guess it's always on my mind, even when I'm not really thinking about it.

There are some things that make it easier. One is that the gang who bothers me on the bus sometimes gets kicked off the bus for a few days—not for going after me, just for being jerks. So then I get a bit of a break. Another is that I have a friend in this area in an older grade at high school. He has a car, and when it's possible, he lets me ride back from school with him.

I'm just wondering if the kids who bully me are getting bullied by their parents. They learn it from somewhere.

I try to stay away from the kids who bother me, but they'll follow me. It feels like they're hunting me. I'll walk away, and they'll come after me. I'll change seats on the bus, and they'll move up to sit where I'm sitting. I've gotten a bit of a break lately because they've started picking on another kid. I know I should stand up for him, but I don't. I need to have their attention off me for a while.

I don't know why these kids aren't kicked off the bus for good. Why should they get to ride it when they behave so badly?

ANONYMOUS GIRL, 17

I'M NOT IN SCHOOL ANYMORE because of bullying. I take courses now by correspondence. The bullying started in grade seven and it got really bad in grade nine.

In grade seven and eight it was just taunting, like, "She's so fat"—nothing too bad. They'd been doing that since grade three, but new kids came in grade seven and made it worse.

I told the teachers sometimes, and I told my mom. The teachers talked to the kids, and it would get better for a while. Then it would start up again.

I was really looking forward to high school. I thought there would be a lot more kids, so they wouldn't be so focused on me and it would be better.

Some of the worst kids from junior high came to the same high school, and they got all their new friends to start in on me. That's when I went to the vice principal and principal about it. They told me they'd take care of it, but they didn't do anything.

It got really bad around grade ten. It got to the point where I couldn't walk down the hallway. I couldn't go to any of my classes. I couldn't go to the cafeteria. When I'd walk into the cafeteria, I'd get sandwiches and garbage thrown at me.

When I'd walk into class, I'd get paper balls and pencils and erasers thrown at me. People would say stuff and call me names.

At lunchtime I took to hiding down a back hallway where nobody was. That's where I spent most of grade ten and eleven—down the back hallway.

Although I made a few friends at the beginning of grade nine, they fell away as the bullying stepped up. I faced it all alone. I didn't feel I could join any clubs because I was sure it would just be more of what I was already getting.

I don't know why I became such a target for so many people. I'd never done anything to them. And a lot of the kids throwing things and calling me names were kids I'd never met.

My mom came to pick me up from school a couple of times and she heard kids take the trouble to stick their heads out the window and call nasty things down at me. It was humiliating, having my mother hear that.

I told the vice principal when it was just a couple of kids and it could have been dealt with. But it spread so much.

One day in math class some guys behind me were calling me names. I could tell that the teacher heard it, but he didn't do anything, so I grabbed my math book and threw it at the kid's head, then I grabbed another book and threw that.

One of the kids later apologized to me. The other kid, the ringleader—I was made to apologize to him for hitting him with the book.

That's when it really took off. This guy got all his friends to make fun of me and throw things at me.

This continued until I left school and started correspondence.

I told many teachers this was going on. I failed most of my classes because I never went. I'd go to school in the morning then go sit in the back hallway and read and look at magazines and wait for the day to end.

Sometimes the teachers let me switch classes, and that would help for a while. But then it would start up again.

None of those teachers would walk into a workplace day after day, month after month, with people calling them names and throwing things at them. But they'd tell me again and again, "Oh, just ignore it."

I didn't want to go to school. In the morning, I'd tell my mom that I didn't want to go. A couple of times, she'd let me stay home. Most of the rest of the time, I'd go but wouldn't go to any of my classes. I'd find places to hide.

Sometimes the principal or a teacher would find

me and force me back into class. But I'd leave as soon as I could.

At my age, I'm supposed to be in grade twelve and have thirty-four credits. I only have nine credits. That's like whole years lost. All that time gone and wasted.

There would be automated messages from the school on our answering machine every night saying I'd missed my classes. I told the teachers why I wasn't going, but still nothing changed.

I had to convince the school board to let me take correspondence courses. I had to go to meetings and provide them with reasons I couldn't go to school. I don't think the school had a problem with me leaving. I think they were probably happy to see me go.

It was such a relief to get out of that school. I'd gotten really bad social anxiety there and I still have it. I hardly ever leave the house. I get physically ill when I go into the town where my old school is.

My mom wanted me to switch schools instead of doing correspondence, and I'd like to go to a school and have friends, but I just can't be around people anymore.

The correspondence courses aren't going so well. I can't concentrate. I've only completed one credit. I just don't see how I'll go forward.

I don't know what kind of life I'm going to have. Am I going to live with my mom and stepdad forever? Will I ever be able to get an education or a job? I just don't want to see anyone.

The funny thing is, I'm following in my family's footsteps. My mom quit high school before she graduated because she was bullied, and my older sister dropped out for the same reason. It's like a legacy. It's what we do.

WHAT DO YOU THINK?

- Were there other choices Anonymous Girl could have made instead of hiding in the back hallways?

- Does her family history of bullying have anything to do with Anonymous Girl's situation?

Life isn't a battle of survival of the fittest, although many seem to think so. If you are being bullied, do not lose your self-esteem. You should always stand up for yourself, but if you feel afraid to do so, talk to a grown-up or someone you trust. Being bullied is not the end of the world. Although it may seem like it, it is a phase and will pass with time. Strength comes from within.

–MICHELLE PANZO, GRADE TWELVE, ANGOLA

ALEXIS, 11

BULLYING HAS BEEN a part of my life for a while. I've been pushed into chairs. Someone spilled stuff on my lap, then went around the school saying I had peed myself.

This stuff didn't happen by accident. Sometimes things just happen by mistake and it's nobody's fault, but this wasn't an accident. In grade six, somebody put sticky stuff all over my chair, and I didn't see it so I sat down and got sticky stuff all over my pants. Another boy put magic marker on my shirts and dabbed paint on me.

All this mostly started in grade five. The same kids would do it—just a couple of kids—over and over. Every week there would be something. They'd call me fat or stupid, or trip me as I walked by to go to the pencil sharpener. Once, someone cut a chunk out of my hair. I've had to throw out some of my clothes because they got ruined by bullies. I've had sharpened pencils jabbed into me. Over and over, these things went on.

All this happened in class, while the teacher was there. I told my teacher about it, and she said that if I had problems I should go and put a red pencil on her desk, like a secret signal I wanted to talk to her. It didn't really work, though. She had a lot of other things to deal with. But I appreciate that she tried.

One day, the bullying was really bad, and I asked the teacher if I could go home early, before anything else bad happened. But she wouldn't let me, so I had to go back to class. Some days, I want to go home even when bad things aren't happening. I'm afraid bad things will start—it's always on my mind. I'm always worried about it.

The bullying didn't get less when I told the teacher. Kids would still come up and punch me and call me a loser and swear at me.

It's hard to even remember going to school without having to deal with bullying. I don't know why they pick on me.

Some weeks, the bullying happens every day. Some weeks, it's just a few times.

My mom can always tell when I've had a bad day because I come home angry. I'll slam things around and fight with my younger brothers. She says I get snappy, which means that I snap at anything she says. I'll come home and cry in my room for hours and beg her to not send me back to school. Days and days go by and I never feel happy.

My mom and I went to have a talk with one of the main bullies and her mom. This girl goes back and forth over whether she wants to be my friend or not. Some days, she'll be really friendly, and other days, she'll pretend that she never liked me. I never know what she'll be feeling about me.

My mom knows her mom, so she thought it would be a good idea to talk to her directly. Her mom hadn't known what her daughter was doing, so she told the girl that she shouldn't do it anymore. But then the girl came back at me, full force. It got worse and worse.

The police were called in when I started coming home with bruises. The day I was punched and pushed into the stack of chairs, the school asked me not to go home and tell Mom and Dad about it. They didn't want my parents coming to school and getting upset, because Mom and Dad had been there before to complain about the bullying.

Mom used to come and get me at lunch so that I wouldn't have to spend too much time at school. She'd walk me to school in the morning, walk me home for lunch then back to school, then walk me home again in the afternoon. This was to

keep kids from bullying me outside school.

When Mom had to work, I'd go to her friend's house for lunch. After I got pushed into the chairs, I was at her friend's, and she could tell something was wrong. That's when I told her that the school had asked me to keep it secret from my parents.

My mom's friend told my parents. My dad went to the school and got my backpack and told the school I wouldn't be going back there. The school put a trespass order against my dad, which means that if he ever goes back there, he could be arrested.

Mom was always calling the school. They probably got tired of hearing from my parents. Kids would go into my desk and ruin my art work, and Mom would complain to the teachers, and the teachers would say they couldn't do anything about it.

Just before my father was given the trespass order, he said that enough was enough, and he didn't want the bullying happening to me anymore. Then he got a phone call from the principal, who yelled and said he'd gotten a trespass order taken out. The school board got involved, and there were all kinds of letters back and forth, and all kinds of meetings.

My mom got in trouble with the school, too, because I was absent a lot. The reason I was absent so much was to give my nerves a rest. I'd get so upset over the bullying that sometimes I was too upset to go to school, so Mom would say I could stay home and calm down.

After all that, my mom and dad decided to home-school me for a while. The school board provided me with a teacher who would come right to my house, just for me, to make sure I did all my schoolwork.

We had a speaker come to our school once to talk about bullying. He said his son had died from being bullied, but the bullying still didn't stop at our school.

I had a lot of trips to the doctor while the bullying was going on, because I'd be bruised and hurt. I had to go to counseling, too, because I felt so bad about myself and so scared all the time. My doctor suggested that my parents should get a lawyer and sue the school because the school was supposed to fix this. I was up most nights, crying hard and unhappy. I'd beg Mom not to make me go to school, and sometimes she couldn't make me; but mostly I had to go because that's the law. Now the doctors say I have an anxiety disorder from all the bullying.

Once the school board heard everything, they really helped and things were made better.

And now I'm in a new school, and things are good. Nobody bullies me, and I've got art and cheerleading, and I'm going to join army cadets. I want to be an artist or a photographer when I grow up. For a while, I wanted to be a nurse like my mom, but nurses work too hard.

Through all of this, one thing I've learned is that I shouldn't believe what other people say when they are saying bad things about me. I should be proud of who I am.

I'm not going to let the bullying hurt the rest of my life. From now on, I'm gong to have a good life. I don't think that I'll have to deal with bullying again. I'm a lot stronger now than I used to be.

WHAT DO YOU THINK?

• Did it help Alexis to have her parents take the situation so seriously?

• What can parents and educators do to get on the same page against bullying?

When I was a newcomer in this school I was bullied by the big girls. They told me to give them my food. They said if I didn't, I would be beaten and have to mop the dormitory. I reported the girls to the matron and they were severely punished. They were also taken to the administration for further punishment.

—NABUKENYA ZAINABU,
THIRTEEN, UGANDA

GARY, 16

IN GRADE FIVE, kids started calling me names at school, names like "faggot" and other racist names. And then there were older boys in the neighborhood who considered my friend and me their younger brothers, which meant they could beat us up whenever they felt like it. And they *really* beat us up, smashing my ribs a couple of times, giving me bloody noses and black eyes. They had a theory that beating us up would make us stronger. And they would laugh when they were doing it, like it was a joke or a game. Sometimes they'd take it too far, and we'd really get hurt.

These beatings would mostly happen on the playground outside where we lived. We'd have to go through the playground to get home, and the older guys would be there, waiting to get us. I'd be kind of scared, but not outrageously, because at the time I believed what they told me—that every beating would make me a little bit stronger. They'd punch me in my ribs, kick me in the back and groin, hold my arms back and hit me in the stomach. Stuff like that. It went on for a few years.

The physical beating was bad, but what was even worse was the humiliation. When I got a little bit older, like maybe grade eight, I'd be sitting on the bench with my girlfriend and they'd come along and beat me up in front of her. I was a small kid and they'd beat me up and say, "Get tough! Get tough!" They'd be laughing. They could see I was getting mad because I didn't want my girlfriend to see me getting beat—and that made them beat harder and laugh harder.

My girlfriend just sat and watched. Fights like that happened a lot, so she was used to it. But after seeing me get beaten, she didn't want to be my girlfriend anymore.

And then I finally started to grow, and I became the one going after other guys.

I only went after guys older and bigger, but I'd catch them when they were alone, without their buddies. I'd get some of my friends together, and we'd all go after one lone bigger guy. We'd spy on him and follow him and when he got to the right kind of place, we'd jump him and beat him badly. He'd be crying, "No! No!" and we'd be laughing and hurting him.

There was a lot of retaliation for sure. They'd ambush us, and back and forth it would go.

That was just the way things went. We had many fights with bigger kids. We had to try to keep our pride.

Like in school, if someone brushes up against you in the halls, you have to decide if it's an accident or if they're trying to test you. And if it's a test, you'd better be ready to fight because if you're not, they'll all start to come after you.

I think all this fighting made me stronger. I can apply all those stupid little moments to my life now, and I can make decisions about how to behave.

I don't think being bullied is that bad a thing. Sure, some people are really hurt by it, but they can become stronger and harder because of it. Once they get over the pain. If they get bullied again, they can handle it with more strength.

That's if you're able to fight. If it's bullying between kids, you can find a way to fight whoever is after you. Maybe you'll come out on top and they'll leave you alone, or maybe you'll get beaten up badly. But at least you'll let them know they can't walk all over you.

But when adults bully kids, that's a different story. How can kids fight back? Adults have all the power, and they have all these things they can use against you, like dreaming up stupid rules—doing things that tell you that you are nothing and they are everything. Being bullied by adults really grinds you down. They don't fight fair, and they don't fight honest.

All the fighting I've done has taught me how to control myself. I know I can fight, so I don't have to keep proving myself. I can have patience when people get on my case—especially adults with too much authority.

Bullies are generally cowards. You're stronger if you don't bully because it means you have self-control and self-respect. You know you don't have anything to prove.

I think bullies are really hurting inside. They have to maintain a hard shell, but it's like an eggshell—easily cracked, and all soft inside. Bullies are just hiding themselves behind this shell, and you just have to call their bluff.

It really works, standing up to a bully. He'll think twice about coming after you again because he might get a punch in the face.

Bullies are normal people, just like the rest of us. They're nothing to be afraid of. You're not going to die from a punch.

What I'd like to do with my life is open a small business, like a corner shop or a family restaurant. I'd like to do something where folks from the neighborhood, all folks, could get together and greet each other and pass some good moments of the day.

WHAT DO YOU THINK?

- Do you think the older kids who beat Gary up really thought they were doing him a favor?

- Do you agree with Gary that "adults don't fight fair, and they don't fight honest"? If so, what are some examples of this? Is there anything you can do when you are faced with adults behaving unfairly?

ANONYMOUS GIRL, 13

I'M THE ONE WHO does the bullying. Nobody dares pick on me.

Me and my friends target this one girl. I'll call her R. She's really strange and annoying, and that's why we go after her.

We'll sit right behind her on the bus and tell her, "We're going to get you," and "We're coming after you"—stuff like that, to make her afraid. We'll tell her how annoying she is, and that we don't want her talking to us or even talking around us. She tries to copy us because she wants to be cool like we are, but she'll never be like us, no matter how hard she tries. It's annoying when she tries.

Everything she does is annoying—how she talks, how she moves, how she behaves. It's all awful. We have to put up with it because she's in our class. We can't get away from her.

Nobody likes her. She tries to dress like the rest of us, but everyone knows her clothes come from the Giant Tiger or the Bargain Shop. Those stores sell clothes that look like cool clothes when you first look at them, but if you see the label you know they're cheap.

She does stuff to try to make herself look better, but it never works, so we just laugh at her when she tries.

She tries to hang out with the popular people, and that really annoys us because we have to stop what we're doing and tell her to get lost. Most of the popular people shop at the good stores, like Hollister Co. and Ardene, and it's annoying when she tries to copy us. Or she'll find a bag from a good store and she'll put her books in it, and say, "Oh, I shop here all the time." But we all know she doesn't.

Her parents don't do anything. Her mom is sick a lot, and her dad is in jail, so she tries to hang out with us so she'll feel happier, but it's not our job to make her happy. We have other things to do. She claims she's sick all the time, with serious things like heart problems. It's pathetic. She just wants people to be nice to her so she makes up these stories, but it doesn't help because we still don't want to be nice to her. We just want her to go away.

We think she stinks, too. She says she showers every day, but we don't see how she can. The house she lives in is such a wreck. It's made up of old tobacco barns or something. It's rotting away, just like she is.

I've known R for a few years. She wasn't always so annoying. In fact, I used to even like her. Then, a couple of years ago, her father started getting violent and hitting and kicking everyone in the house. He got arrested and R got awful.

I found new friends around that time—cool friends, friends I didn't have to be embarrassed about—so I certainly didn't want to hang out with her anymore.

My new friends are really popular. We're the tough girls, the ones the other kids are afraid of. R is our main target, but we're always going after others, too. If they don't respect us, we need to stand up for ourselves. I feel good when I go after other kids. I mean, I don't do it just to make them feel bad, but I'd feel bad if I let them annoy me and I didn't do anything about it.

My grandmother doesn't like me hanging out with my new friends. She doesn't think they're good for me because they smoke and drink, but she doesn't know. She thinks they've made me more aggressive. But it's not them—it's other people, the annoying people.

Like, we went into town a couple of months ago—we live out in the country—just to go to a friend's house and go to the stores, just for something to do. My grandmother dropped us off. We went to visit this one girl, and there was another girl already there that I didn't like. Our friends made us fight each other.

My friends said, "She said nasty things about you. You have to go after her." And her friends flicked cigarettes and gum at my head. And she had me backed into a corner of her yard, by the fence.

There was no way out, so I had to fight. She punched me in the face, and lunged at me. My nose snapped—I heard it. She broke my nose! It really hurt. She had me on the ground. She had hold of me by the hair and was pounding my head on the ground. My brother was the one who finally pulled her off and got me out of the house.

I had to go to the emergency department. They thought I had a concussion. My eyes got all black and bruised, and I had all these headaches.

I don't care. My friends and I fight other girls all the time. When there aren't any other girls around to fight, we'll fight each other, for practice. It's something to do out in the country.

I get detentions a lot. Often it's for bugging R. I don't care. I just sit in the detention room and talk to my friends. We're supposed to write out stupid lines, so we do that fast, then just hang around and talk. Detention is a joke.

People say I should be nicer to R. My friends and I hang out at these picnic tables when the weather is good and R always wants to hang out there with us. The principal says I should give her a chance because she has a hard life.

Well, my life is hard, and no one is being nice to me. My mother lives in one town with her boyfriend and my father lives in another town with his girlfriend. I live with my grandmother and my brother and younger sister. My parents try to tell me what to do, but I don't have to listen to them. They can't control me.

My grandmother can't control me, either. She has to fight to get me to school every day because I don't want to get out of bed. I don't want to face it. It gives me stomachaches. School is just bad grades and teachers telling me to be nice to kids I don't like. It's useless.

There are some good things in my life. I like to dance, hip-hop. I don't take lessons. I don't need lessons. I know how to do it already.

I used to like going on the Internet, but Gran took the computer away because I was using it to go after other kids. But I'll get it back someday. If I'm bored at home, I'll go after my little sister, who gets good grades and really annoys me. My brother and I go after her together.

I don't know what I'll do with my life. Probably be a hairdresser. Who cares? I don't.

WHAT DO YOU THINK?

• Why do you think Anonymous Girl acts the way she does?

• What do you think it would take to get her to change?

Bullying is worse than anything you can imagine. It's like you're in a world full of enemies without any place to go. There are lots of children who turn into bullies because their parents are like that. Some children have family problems, so they ease their own sadness a little by making others sad. These bullies should be comforted, and then they might even stop bullying. If you see someone being bullied, please stand up for them before they turn into bullies themselves

–KASUNI WICKRAMASINGHE, GRADE SIX, SRI LANKA

Talking About

WE WANT TO CRUSH YOU

In each of the interviews in this section, kids have talked about the terrible toll bullying has taken on their lives. But things did not get this bad overnight. The present day is built on the past. Decisions we made yesterday affect what we do today. If the right steps had been taken earlier on, these kids would all be living very different lives now.

- What decisions have you made in the past that affect your life now, for good or for bad?

- What does it mean to humiliate someone? Have you ever felt humiliated? Do adults ever humiliate children? What can you do when you see this happening?

- When someone is chronically bullied by a lot of people, do teachers get tired of hearing about it? What do you think teachers can do to put a stop to this kind of bullying?

- What difference does it make in your life to have at least one good friend? What do you look for in a good friend? Are you a good friend to somebody?

- How do people who bully get other kids to go along with them?

Sometimes people bully because they were bullied. Sometimes their dads were bullies and their dads bullied them, and that's how they came to be bullies

–MATTHEW YAMAMOTA,
GRADE TWO, JAPAN

PART FIVE

REDEMPTION

Redemption means to reclaim ourselves, to right what is wrong, to be free from the bondage of an injustice we have done or that has been done to us.

When we replace the negative messages bullying has put into our heads with messages of courage and joy, we experience redemption. When we find ways to deal with our anger and frustration without hurting others, we find redemption. And when we can build ourselves up without tearing others down, redemption is ours.

In this section, the kids interviewed tell us about their own moments of redemption, when they begin to take their lives back from bullying.

ANONYMOUS BOY, 17

I'M GOING INTO GRADE ELEVEN. Bullying has been a part of my life ever since I started school. That's eleven years, including kindergarten.

When I was three, I was already reading at a grade-one level. Kids started picking on me when they found out I was smart. It got worse when they found out I wasn't athletic.

I have a mild form of cerebral palsy. You don't notice it right away when you first meet me, but I'm very uncoordinated. My balance isn't great and I'm always tripping over my own feet. Gym class was awful. The kids who couldn't do things were ridiculed by other kids and by the teacher.

It became a game for kids to push me and shove me at recess. I fell down easily so they thought it was funny even though I told them it wasn't. I remember trying to fight them off in grade one. If there were too many to fight, or if I wasn't feeling strong that day, I'd run away and hide.

In a small town, the same kids will go to the same school for years. There's not a lot of moving in and out. So if a kid gets away with being a jerk in grade one or two, chances are he's just going to become better at being a jerk by the time he's in grade eight. Nobody gets a fresh start.

My life continued this way all through the school.

Kids saw me as someone to go after. Mostly it was the same bunch of kids who would target me, led by one particular kid that nobody bothered to stop.

They did all kinds of things to me. They'd push my head between the bars of the playground equipment. They'd steal or break my possessions, rip up my completed homework, tear my clothes, poke me with pens, or blow on the back of my neck during class if they sat behind me. They'd break off pieces of eraser and whip them at me. Crazy stuff—stuff adults would not put up with from other adults.

Sometimes I'd tell the teachers and sometimes some of them would try to do something, but it never really changed. The teachers would end up annoyed with me for still having the problem.

The teachers who had been teaching for a long time were generally better than the new teachers. New teachers are afraid of lawsuits, I think, or they're afraid of the kids complaining to their parents, the parents complaining to the board, and then the teachers getting into trouble.

Nobody feels backed up to deal with the problem, so the problem continues.

Mrs. Gillespie was a really great teacher. She was very strict and very fair, and she didn't put up with any crap in her classroom. I had her for the afternoons of grade seven and for two months in grade eight. It was great. In her class, no one threatened me or insulted me or pushed me or damaged my work. They knew if they did, they would be in serious trouble. She didn't yell or make kids scared. She just expected everyone to behave and she wasn't afraid of anyone.

Outside of class, it was business as usual. Nothing happened to the kids doing the bullying. The principal had this idea that if kids did less than three offences a week, the next week their slate was wiped clean. So as long as they were only caught twice in one week, nothing happened to them.

Except for in Mrs. Gillespie's class, kids would attack each other right in front of the teacher, and the teacher would pretend not to notice. If you don't see, you don't have to do anything, right? I remember being in class one day, kids throwing things at me and hitting me—and the teacher watching and not stopping it. So I just walked out.

Some of the stuff that happens is really dumb and unnecessary. When I got to high school, I was assigned a locker right in between the two boys that bullied me the most in grade school. What are the chances? It took a lot of phone calls from my parents to get that changed.

One of the meanest things that ever happened to me was done by a girl. People think guys are the mean ones, but girls can be just as terrible.

I was invited to a school dance, like a formal, by a girl who was a lot more popular than me. I thought,

finally, all this is over and I'm going to have friends! She bragged about it all over the school, about how she and I were going to the dance together.

I got a haircut, new clothes, and got all dressed up. My mom said I looked really good.

The plan was to meet her at the school. My mom dropped me off and I waited for my date in the foyer, like we'd arranged. Finally, she walks in on the arm of another guy and says to me, really loud so everyone could hear, "I can't believe you thought I would go out with you!" And she started to laugh and tell everyone what a loser I was.

The guy who was her date hadn't known anything about this. He even apologized to me.

What was she thinking? That this would make her look smarter, or prettier? It didn't. I hope that's a moment she regrets for the rest of her life.

I stayed at the dance. I didn't have a ride home, and my pride wouldn't let me call home to get picked up early. For four hours, I stayed at the dance, with folks laughing at me and pointing at me. I pretended it didn't bother me. When Mom picked me up and I got into the van and closed the door, that's when I started to cry.

Mom has called the office at the schools I've gone to so often that she's been labeled a paranoid parent. Well, they found out last March that she's not paranoid.

Remember, this had been going on, almost unchecked, for years and years.

I do have a couple of close friends at school, and one of the ways we communicate is to pass a journal back and forth.

Well, I was so fed up that I started venting in the journal about what jerks these guys were, and what I'd like to do to them to pay them back. I made a list of all their names. I wasn't really going to do anything to them, but it made me feel more powerful to imagine it. I won't go into details about what I imagined—just that it involved fixing it so that these kids wouldn't bother me anymore.

I called it an Avoidance List. The police called it a Hit List, maybe because I also put down a date, May 13, and said that was the date for the Final Solution.

My friend got freaked out by this, showed the journal to her father, and he showed it to other people, who read it before I could explain exactly what it was.

The next thing I knew, I was in the seclusion room at the local hospital.

All this happened on the same day my mom had major surgery at a hospital in a nearby city. She had a full hysterectomy. That's serious. She and my dad had just gotten back to her room from the recovery room when they were asked to call the school about their son. They thought my brother had gotten into another fight. The school had never called them about me before.

The next day, I was transferred to the mental health ward in Brantford. I was held in seclusion and guarded by police.

No charges were laid, and I was cleared by both a child psychologist and an adult psychologist. They both said I was not a threat to myself or others.

I was out of school for a week, and I had to take in a letter saying I was psychologically fit to be in school.

The message I got out of all this is never to ask for help. It's pointless because nobody does anything. I'll find a way to deal with it myself. I'm learning how to meditate, and to get rid of those bad emotions.

That Avoidance List incident is now in my file. It will follow me when I apply for college, and when I apply for scholarships and grants. I've been on the honor roll for years, but scholarship folks look at more things than grades. They also want to know that the kid they're giving their money to is not going to blow up or cause them problems down the line. So I'm trying to get lots of positive stuff in my file to balance it out.

Bullying just doesn't affect the kids. It affects the parents of the kids being bullied. I've watched Mom and Dad trying their best to get something good happening in the schools for me and my little brother, who started to get picked on because he is my brother. My parents get more and more frustrated because it seems like nobody listens. The parents of kids who are doing the bullying have got to be open to hearing that their baby isn't the precious little darling they like to think he is. Like, maybe their baby is a thug.

Kids who are being bullied should speak up. I feel a little hypocritical saying that, because I don't always speak up. Now, I'm just trying to get through it and get out in one piece.

I have a lot of things in my life that make me feel good about myself, and that helps me feel better when I'm bullied. Like, I'm growing my hair long now so I can cut it off in grade twelve and donate it to Locks of Love, which helps people with cancer. I'm a peer tutor. I'm involved in filmmaking, and I'm going to be filming a local commercial for a fish-and-chips shop. I play base, keyboard, electric guitar, clarinet, saxophone, tuba, and drums. I helped rebuild a race car. I used to race dirt bikes until I broke my leg. I have a truck-polishing business, too. I have a lot going on.

My family is important to me. My brother gets bullied, too, but he deals with it differently from me. He lets it roll off him until he's had enough, then he lets the bully have it. It gets him into trouble, but the kids don't bug him so much. My father is a long-haul truck driver, and my mother has multiple sclerosis. Some days for her are harder than others. When she's feeling good, she races hot rods at the Cayuga drag races. When she's having a bad day, the chores fall to us. We all have to pitch in together as a family to make it work, and I like being an important part of that.

With all this good stuff in my life, I'm going to succeed in spite of what's happened to me. I wonder if the kids who have bullied me will be so lucky.

WHAT DO YOU THINK?

- Anonymous Boy felt safe in Mrs. Gillespie's class. What was it about her classroom that allowed him to feel safe?

- What do you have in your life that helps you feel good about yourself, no matter what else is going on around you?

BRUCE, 16

WHEN I WAS YOUNGER, I lived in a rough neighborhood. All the kids used to beat me up. But when I got bigger and older, I became the one doing the bullying.

When I was small, they'd chase me off basketball courts, steal my money, steal my chips. It all happened outside of school because the teachers were really strict and didn't put up with anything like that. They made school a safe place for me. But outside, I was always in danger.

I got bigger in grade eight, and then I was the one taking kids' money and beating them up. I went after kids who were younger and smaller than me. I didn't care that I was hurting them because I'd been hurt and I figured it was my turn to be on top. I felt strong and confident when I took someone's money or jacket, or whatever. I took things I didn't really need or want, and I would often throw them away into the dirt right after. It wasn't the things I was after. I wanted to feel powerful. It was the taking, not the having.

When I was bullied, I never told anyone because I didn't want to be a rat. My cousins came around sometimes, and they were big and they protected me. But they weren't around all the time. They told me it was better to get beat up and keep my mouth shut than to run around and tell someone because then I'd always be known as a rat, and no one would help me.

My dad was in prison most of the time. My mom worked from seven in the morning until six at night. After school was the most dangerous time for me. That's when I'd get beat up and have my money or candy stolen. There was no safe place to go, no youth center, no parks that were safe from them.

I played sports as much as I could because I was safe there. There were coaches and rules. I escaped into drawing and painting, but I couldn't let anyone see me doing that because they'd use it as a reason to beat me.

I'd like to be a tattoo artist. I designed some of the tattoos I've got on my arms. I'd like to be a welder, too. I did some welding in grade nine. I really liked it. As an artist, I could take welding to a whole new level.

In grade eight I started hanging out with older kids, seventeen- and eighteen-year-old kids. We'd smoke weed, drink, skip school. Adults would sometimes try to tell me I was going down the wrong path, but I paid no attention to them. The only thing that might have made an impression was if a cop had come and said right to my face that I was this close to getting charged and sent to jail. Anything less, I didn't care.

I had no mentors, just my friends, and they were not looking out for me.

It would have helped if I could have visited my dad in prison, but he was far away in another part of the province. I talked to him on the phone a few times, but I never told him bad stuff. He never knew what was really going on with me, so he couldn't help. We never had real conversations. I'd just say, "I love you and I want you home." It was expensive to phone, and Mom worked all the time just to pay our ordinary bills. We're not letter writers, so those little phone calls were all we had.

I think it would have made a difference if I could have seen him sometimes, enough times to get comfortable really talking to him. I'm not making excuses for myself, but it would have helped if I could have known he was watching out for me even from prison. But it was like we both got sentenced, you know?

Mom had a really hard time with me when I was bullying kids and doing drugs. She had to work all the time or we'd be out on the street, so she couldn't supervise me properly. She kept threatening to call Children's Aid on me if I didn't shape up, and then one day she did call them. She couldn't take care of me.

I was sent to a group home, but I didn't like it there so I ran away. I lived by myself for a year when I was fourteen to fifteen. I found a small apartment in someone's basement. It wasn't a proper apartment—the owners could have been charged because it wasn't built properly. It was a dump, really, so the landlord was glad to take my cash and not ask any questions. I paid the rent by selling drugs and working as a roofer.

I didn't go to school. I'd gone in grade nine when I was living at home, but in the first month of grade ten I got kicked out for Tasering some kids. I bought the Taser off a friend, for protection. I don't know where he got it, but it's possible to buy just about anything.

I did everything for myself when I lived on my own—did my laundry, went grocery shopping, made my meals. I was lonely a lot, and I always felt under pressure because I was doing things that were illegal just to make money for rent. I know I wasn't paid properly at a lot of the jobs I did because it wasn't legal to hire me. They paid me under the table, so they cheated me. But there was nothing I could do about that. Bullies. Older kids when I was younger and adults when I got older. I was always dealing with bullies.

But I kept it up. I found out later that a Missing Persons Report was out on me, but I managed to stay away.

Then the whole thing just fell apart because I couldn't get any more work. Places wouldn't hire me because I was underage and I couldn't present any identification. I got more and more afraid of selling drugs because I didn't want to get caught. It's a hard way to live.

Mom knew I was all right but she didn't know where I was. I phoned her a few times, and she told me to go back to the group home, but I didn't like the rules there.

It would have helped me a lot, I think, if I'd had a supervised, safe place to go when I was younger—where I could do art and activities and maybe get a snack because I was always so hungry after school. The money I took off other kids I usually used to buy food. So if there had been a place like that, I would have felt strong enough in myself not to go after other kids, not to cause all that trouble for my mother and all that.

Some one-on-one time might have worked, too. And if my mom's job had paid a little more, she wouldn't have had to work such long hours and she'd have been better able to watch out for me.

It still all comes down to me. A lot of kids have it rough and they don't beat up folks or steal from them.

But you asked me what would have helped, and I think all that would have.

Things are going much better now. I have a good relationship with my mom and I'm back in school. My reading is improving, and I've calmed down a lot. The bad period in my life is over now.

WHAT DO YOU THINK?

- What effect did it have on Bruce to have his father in prison?

- School was a safe place for Bruce. What makes a school a safe place?

Bullies are lonely people. They don't have friends because they don't know how to make friends. So bullies do bad things to get attention. We can make bullies into our good friends. We can care about them.

–SORA YOON,
GRADE TWO, SOUTH KOREA

KATIE, 16

I'VE ALWAYS LIVED in the house I live in now.

I no longer go to public school. I left it a little over a year ago, at the end of grade nine. I left because I couldn't stand the bullying.

It had been going on as long as I was in school, since the first day of kindergarten. I was obviously very nervous, and all the other kids would just stop and stare and leave me out of games. As the school year went on, that escalated into pushing me and knocking me down. I still have scars on my knees from being pushed down during that time.

There are so many reasons why kids have chosen to target me. My dad's a long-distance truck driver.

My mom is physically disabled. I had just come back from vacation and was really tanned. The kids at school just found everything possible to comment on. Every part of my life was something they ridiculed. At one point I had my hair cut really short, then I grew it out. They picked on me for growing it long, then when I cut it short again, they laughed at me about that, too.

Over the years, there were so many things. They made fun of me because I didn't have a boyfriend, because I didn't wear makeup, because I didn't have brand-name clothes. You name it. Anything.

At first I was really surprised by what they were doing. I thought school was a good thing to go to. I loved learning—I'd been reading since I was three—and I expected school to be amazing. It turned out to be horrible. I absolutely hated it. I cried every night.

At the beginning, I used to cry right at school. I soon learned that crying made things worse, so I stopped doing that. I told everyone over the years what was going on—teachers, parents, principal, police—but nothing was done.

As the kids got bigger, the attacks got more vicious and more serious. They even tried killing me. They tried breaking my arm. The police did reports, they interviewed people, but months would go by and nothing would happen. The bullying would go on. My mom called the police to ask what was going on, and the police said they weren't pressing charges because they didn't want to upset the families of the kids involved.

It's a small town. It's a last-name town. Some of the last names go way back, and if you have any of those last names then you're like town royalty. You have higher social status.

My family is on the low end of the town's hierarchy. Even though I was born here, my parents came from away. My mother was born in Barbados and lived all over Canada before she came here, and my father's parents are from Germany. So we're outsiders.

I did have a friend at school for one year. She was wonderful—she'd intervene for me when someone was going to slug me. But she moved away after that one year.

I had another friend I'd known since we were babies. We were friends at school at the beginning, then one day she suddenly wanted to break my arm. I didn't see that coming. She just decided one day that she was going to attack me and not be friends with me anymore. Looking back, I can see where she'd been acting weird and unfriendly before that. But at the time, I didn't see it.

The bullying went on all through school. Even some of the teachers would bully me. But in grade eight, one teacher recognized how bad things were. She even hid me in her classroom so I could escape from the kids who were attacking me. The bully in this case was saying bad things should happen to me because I wasn't a proper Christian, and she'd steal stuff from me and threaten me. She was bullying me online, too, sending threats and insults. So the teacher hid me.

The end to that bullying came when we graduated from grade eight and didn't have to see each other so much anymore. But she made friends with kids who were friends with me in grade nine, and she turned them against me. It was horrible. I had finally gotten into a group with some girls who liked me, and the group cast me out.

Part of it was, I think, jealousy. I started up an anti-bullying Web site while I was still going to school. My friends complained that I was spending too much time on it and ignoring them, which I wasn't.

It was a lot of things, really. I think at the core of it was that I got what I wanted. I'd always wanted my life to have a story, to have something special I did make a difference, to make my life worth living. And I found it through the Web site.

But the Web site, talking about the existence of bullying, pointed out that life in our little town was not all lovely. Growing up is not a fairy tale. It can be awful. And maybe they didn't want these things pointed out, because that took away all the things they thought about their lives.

I don't know for sure. It just got bad.

I've had so many injuries done to me from bullying that I've been diagnosed with Complex Regional Pain Syndrome. Kids even almost broke my back. My skull has been injured. And all the stress has made everything worse.

Sometimes I knew the kids who bullied me. Sometimes it seemed completely random. In grade eight, I was walking quickly along the street because I was late for math class. Two guys saw me and said, "Let's hurt her." They shoved me into their friends. One of their elbows went right into my temple, and they all laughed.

Mom practically lived at the school, in the principal's office. Eventually the school apologized to us for something, but an apology doesn't mean very much. What about handing out real punishments to the kids who bully?

Every now and then we'd have bullying assemblies, but all they seemed to do was teach the bullies how to get away with it.

I was in grade seven when some kids threw rocks at me right on the playground. Their punishment was to stay in during recess, which didn't seem like anything. I went home crying that day, then Mom brought me into the principal's office. Mom said, "Katie should be the one to decide their punishment." We talked about it, and what I came up with was that all the rocks should be swept off the tarmac. And the principal went along with it. For two days, the kids spent their recess sweeping the rocks off the playground. They had to apologize to me, too. It was a punishment that made sense. I felt good about that.

That principal was great. He didn't put up with any nonsense. He let me switch classes when kids in one class were going after me. He let me work in the office during phys ed, since a lot of bullying happened there.

I finally left school because I got tired of all the bullying and of the teachers doing nothing to stop it. Our school was running at 130 percent capacity. The halls were always packed, and the teachers couldn't control what was going on. And things kept happening. Some kids tried to throw me down stairs. So many things.

Because of all these attacks, my old injuries from other bullying never healed properly. My arm is still messed up so bad. I can't play my guitar or my violin. I wear a brace on my back. I get terrible headaches from the neck injuries. Even now, since leaving school, I'm sick probably once a week from the stress.

I stopped going to school when I was fifteen. I wrote my final grade-nine exam in June, and I walked through the door of my house and told my mother, "I'm not going back." And Mom said, "Fine." She had had enough, too.

I do school online now. It's a better way of doing school. It might take me a little longer, but I study at my own pace and I don't have to worry about other kids.

And I work on my Web site. It's a Web site about bullying by youth and for youth. I co-founded it with Robert, a kid in New Brunswick who'd been bullied all his life because he has cerebral palsy. The Web site has a sponsor, and we get hundreds of hits a day. The Web site is www.bullyingcanada.ca.

We want the Web site to be where everyone can come, even the kids doing bullying, and we'll be there with them until the problem is solved. We need to treat people who bully not as bad people but as people who need help. We need to walk beside them and not judge them.

It's hard to be going through this in a small town. Even though I don't go to school anymore, when I leave the house I'm always worried that I'll run into one of the kids who bullied me. So I usually stay inside. We might move to another part of the country when I'm done high school, but that's still a few years away.

The Web site has saved my life, really. It's given me a reason to keep going.

- By creating a Web site, Katie has turned a terrible experience into a positive service that can help others. What other ideas might work?

- Why do you think Katie was able to overcome her experience, instead of becoming mean herself?

LEN, 15

I WAS A BULLY when I was younger, starting in grade four. I'd push the kids around, beat them up, take their money—stuff like that. It made me feel bigger, more important than everyone else.

In grade four, I got a growth spurt which made me physically bigger than the other kids. Bullying them made me feel emotionally bigger, too.

I learned it all from my older brothers. They were always beating me up when I was small and stealing from me, slapping me around. Sometimes I'd tell my dad and they'd get into trouble. Dad would yell at them or hit out at them, then they'd come back and beat me up worse.

When I'd beat up kids at school, I'd warn them not to tell the teachers, and mostly they wouldn't. When they did, I'd get hauled down to the principal's office. He'd ask me what I did and why I did it. Sometimes I'd lie my way out of it. Sometimes I'd get detention or an in-school suspension, which was a joke. I'd just go sit in the office and read.

None of that stopped me. You see, now I'd have to go after the kids who told on me and hurt them more as a warning to others. I couldn't let them get away with it.

I went after the kids in my class. I didn't really like them. They were loser kids—the way they dressed, the way their hair looked, the way they talked.

I didn't go after my friends. We would all go after the loser kids together. It was fun to see that we bothered them, that they were sitting there afraid of us. It made us feel powerful and it cut down on our boredom.

None of them ever stood up for themselves. If they had tried, we would have picked on them worse. If they had persisted, maybe stood up to us every day for two weeks, we would have gotten the message, but they never did stand up to us. Or if they did, they'd stop after the first, "Leave me alone!" so we knew they weren't serious about it.

I'd hit kids all the time. It wouldn't have stopped me if they'd hit me back because I was bigger and they'd never be able to hurt me. Besides, I'm used to being hit. It's nothing. It's just being hit.

Everyone made fun of these kids. When I joined in, it just made me more popular. The punishments I got were a joke. Why would I stop bullying? I didn't know anything about these kids except that they looked funny—and that was enough of a reason for me to go after them.

It was fun to take stuff off them and watch them cry. Especially when I knew it was something they'd worked hard for or their parents had given them.

Teachers can be bullied, too. Some kids think that teachers have all the power, but if you're as big as they are and you don't care what they do to you, you can make their life hell at school. I've seen teachers who were afraid of me. So when they're walking down the hall and I'm stealing stuff from a kid who's crying, they'll keep on walking and look the other way so I don't come after them.

All it took to make teachers afraid of me was to freak out a couple of times. I lost my temper, threw a desk or two, and from then on they were afraid.

I didn't stop behaving like this until grade eight. The kids I'd been bullying had grown over the summer. They'd filled out and they weren't so scared anymore. It was a waste of time picking on them. It wasn't any fun anymore, so why bother?

High school was bigger, and even the losers had friends. Picking on them would have grown into a much bigger deal with more and more kids involved, and I had other things to do. I was one of the cool kids—tough, dressed properly, like that—and we hung out together and ignored everyone else.

I probably wouldn't have picked on the loser kids if I'd known something about them. As it was, they weren't really people to me. If I'd known what they were inside, what they did when they weren't at school, what they were trying to be good at, I probably wouldn't have gone after them, because you don't go after people you respect. If I could have known their families, too, it might have made them seem more like me—like if they had brothers who beat on them or parents who insulted them. We'd have things in common, and we could be friends.

Some sort of group to get us all together to learn about each other might have helped. If we'd been made to sit down and talk to a kid we didn't know and find out what they were all about, then we wouldn't have seen them as strangers. They'd have been real people. But we'd never do that on our own because we had to look after ourselves and our reputations.

I don't know if I'll bully others when I become an adult or not. We do what works, right? I like to think I'll have the skills to be able to make a good life for myself without bullying. I read a lot of biographies and try to learn from others how to be a better person.

WHAT DO YOU THINK?

- Do you agree with Len that if he had known something about the kids he bullied that he wouldn't have bullied them?

- Do you agree that Len's definition of a loser is one that other people share?

You must embrace courage and have absolute determination that you are going to stop bullying. Others tend to fall back and just watch. They don't want to get into the situation, so they hesitate. You can't just see the prey get hunted by the predator. You have to stop it. You have to be heroes.

—SUBARU YOKOTA,
GRADE ELEVEN, JAPAN

SCOTT, 15

ALL THROUGH MY LIFE I've been bullied, and I've bullied others. It's been like the survival of the fittest. You get picked on, you see other people being picked on, and you start picking on people, too. You see other people doing it and you don't really want to be the target. It takes some pressure off you if you put it onto someone else.

Mostly I was the target of verbal bullying and name-calling. Other kids said I was dressed funny. People with less money get made fun of a lot. My family wasn't very well off, but I was the only child so my family could afford to keep me from looking too poor, especially my grandparents. But other kids had it rougher.

When I look back on it now I wonder what in the world I was thinking, making fun of poor kids. Not only did these kids have it rough because their dads were out of work or their moms were drunks or whatever, but we added insult to injury by making fun of them for things that were not their fault. I behaved like a jerk.

Bullying happens everywhere, even at work. I worked in an auto shop for a while. Two adults, forty-year-old men, kept at each other until it turned into a full-blown fight.

I remember this one kid, Jim, in elementary

school. Everyone went after him—the whole school. He smelled. His family was dirt poor. His parents delivered the free shopping news around town, so you know they didn't have anything. I'll call them Jim and Janet, but that's not their real names. Everybody targeted Jim and his little sister Janet. Even me.

One time, I put an open fruit cup in Jim's backpack. Why did I do that? I was young and I thought it made me look like a big man in front of my peers. It worked, too. They thought I was very cool, and at the time, I felt quite good about it. I look back and think how stupid and mean it was. If I'd put myself in his shoes for a second, maybe I wouldn't have done it.

But at the time, it felt like a victory. I even felt brave, coming up with the idea, sneaking over to his bag—heart pumping in case a teacher came by—dumping the fruit cup in and then running away. Like I'd just performed a dangerous, important mission. All my friends were like, "Way to go!" and laughing about the mess in the bag.

Jim and Janet were picked on a lot in school. Constantly. The teachers saw it obviously, and they'd say, "Stop picking on them," but it's like they were the accepted targets, and none of the teachers ever really tried to change that. At least, not that I could see. It was, like, "Yeah, yeah, you shouldn't pick on them, but they bring it on themselves," type of thing.

I don't know what Janet and Jim could have done to stop being targets. Try to fit in better, maybe. Dress better. They smelled. It wasn't their fault. They were growing up kind of different. They lived in a rundown house. Money was obviously a factor.

But that was them. They kind of accepted their roles and they never fought back.

I think it got better for them in high school. They each found a couple of friends. As we get older, we have more power to dress ourselves and keep ourselves clean, and to run our own lives. All that helped them.

Sometimes Jim would try to fight back. He'd say, "Stop that, stop that!" But he had a funny voice, and that would egg us on even more. I think things were too far gone to ever really stop. It was set that he was the one getting made fun of—that was his job. It might have helped if he'd fought back, like if he'd flung himself at us, but he'd been beaten up a lot—although never, thank goodness, by me. That's one thing in my favor. Kids would think nothing of ganging up on him and chasing him and pounding on him. So he was kind of defenseless. All us kids against just him and his sister.

It's really sad when I think about it now. Going after him made me feel so big and important when I was young, but now I can see it made me small and not worth very much.

If I'd been friends with Jim as a kid, I would have been picked on, too. Now, I think I could handle it. As you get older, you realize some things are worth suffering for, and to be a good man who can look the world in the eye without shame is one of those things. But when you are a little kid, your whole life is governed by fear: fear of losing friends, fear of getting into trouble, fear of being made fun of. It's hard to feel strong when you're a little kid.

So I tried to stay as far away from him as I could by making fun of him.

Even when Jim and Janet tried to fit in—like, after Christmas, if they came to school in a sweater that was new and not dirty—we'd just make fun of them for that. They couldn't win.

We went to his house one time. It was kind of a joke. There were six of us in grade seven, a mix of guys and girls. We did it because we were curious about his house, what he lived like. He was glad to see us because we were acting like we were his friends, so he invited us in. His parents weren't there, just him and his sister. He lived with his mom and grandmother, and he would swear about his dad and say he hoped his dad was dead. His dad was some kind of a violent thug. It was a rough situation. Just talking about it now makes me realize how much I made his situation even harder.

The house was a pigsty. Garbage all over, cats tied up, cat poo on the rugs, old food, terrible smells, dirty clothes everywhere. Dust. Grime. Look, if you're a parent and you're poor, you can still keep your place clean. You can keep your kids clean. Have some pride. Don't hurt your kids like that. You can do better.

We used our visit to his house against him. We told everyone what filth he lived in. We egged the outside of his house. The girls who came with us were really upset—more about the way the cats were being looked after than the way Jim and Janet were being looked after. They wanted to tell the teachers or even the police.

It made me feel sorry for Jim and his sister, but not sorry enough to stop bullying them.

Growing up changed me. When you get older and you get more control of your life, you can see things clearer. You can say, "What's the point of behaving this way? What am I gaining from it?" You already have the respect of your peers, so you don't really need to make fun of people anymore. Or you find other ways to get your friends' respect.

I'm not that horrible kid anymore. The bully doesn't have to stay a bully forever. He can change his ways. That should give us all hope.

If you're a kid who's picking on other kids, ask yourself if that's really who you want to be. You'll be a lot stronger if you can show some compassion. Sit down and break bread with the kid you've been bullying. You might learn something.

WHAT DO YOU THINK?

- Do you think Scott's suggestions would help kids who bully feel more sympathy toward the kids they target, and then less likely to bully them?

- Scott talks about some of his past behavior with shame and embarrassment. Are there things you have done that you now wish you hadn't?

The first time I bullied was in pre-kindergarten. I changed in the end because I realized it wasn't nice to hurt people. It wasn't even really fun. I wouldn't have any friends if I kept on doing it. So I chose to stop bullying and become a normal girl.

If you bully others, you should realize that it's not a happy thing to do. You have to stop and take the time to get to know a person. I took the time to change, and I don't bully anyone anymore.

–YARA AKBARALY,
GRADE FIVE, MADAGASCAR

Talking About
REDEMPTION

Redemption means reclaiming our lives from fear, from shame, from frustration. The kids interviewed in this section have all come through the despair of bullying to find new lives for themselves, where they feel calm, in control of themselves, and able to reach out to others.

• How can kids who have been bullied for a long time learn to trust and feel comfortable around people again?

• If you are someone who bullies others, what would it take for you to feel comfortable enough with yourself that you no longer went after other people?

• What sort of supports and programs can be created in your school to help everyone move beyond bullying?

Once I was bullied, but I never showed a sad or angry face to others. I always smiled and tried my best to make them happy. Then slowly I started getting some friends, and I was bullied no more. Don't be ashamed to do this and don't give up. Walk forward, not back.

–JAE JIN LEE,
GRADE SEVEN, KOREA

CONCLUSION

The kids in this book have a lot to say. It was a privilege to meet with them and their families, and to listen to the everyday heroes who do their best to stand up to bullying and create safe spaces.

Bullying is not inevitable. It doesn't have to be a normal part of childhood. The more we talk with each other, share our stories, and listen—particularly to those whose voices aren't often heard—the closer we move toward a just society. We can find ways to support each other, learn from each other, and create a world where we all feel welcome and respected.

Recognizing the power to choose is enlightening, even revolutionary. How we choose to behave with our family, friends, and community influences the sort of world we inherit. Respecting others and respecting ourselves leads naturally to respecting the world and all who live in it. We don't have to settle for what we've learned so far. We can all learn more, reach further, and become the great people we were all meant to be.

When I was young, I was always the third person, the one who watched the bully and the victim but never had the guts to stand up and shout, "Stop it!" Instead, I would try as hard as I could to avoid the victim's eyes, pleading for help. To get rid of these feelings of guilt, I would say to myself, "I'm just a child, I can't do anything." And isn't this how most students excuse themselves for not standing up against the strong? But is there really nothing we can do about it?

One drop of water does not affect a thing when it falls, but a tsunami can sweep the whole city of Tokyo. Like water, humans who act together can have extreme power to overcome bullying. If you are afraid to stand up and be courageous, why don't you gather up your friends and form a tsunami? You can also call teachers or close adults to make an even stronger tsunami. As more and more drops of water join together and form bonds, they will be powerful enough to save people from bullying. You no longer should say, "I'm weak and useless," but rather, "Alone, I may be weak, but with all these helpers, I am strong."

–SOH YEON PAK,
GRADE TEN, SOUTH KOREA

RESOURCES

FOR PARENTS

Coloroso, Barbara.
The Bully, the Bullied and the Bystander.
New York: Harper Collins, 2003

GOVERNMENT OF ALBERTA
CHILDREN AND YOUTH SERVICES
BULLYING PREVENTION STRATEGY
Bullying Prevention Helpline:
    1-888-456-2323
www.child.alberta.ca/home/586.cfm

BULLY BEWARE
    6 Bedingfield St.
    Port Moody, BC V3H 3N1
    1-888-552-8559
www.bullybeware.com

NO BULLY
    3389 22nd St.
    San Francisco, CA 94110
    415-820-3956
www.nobully.com/parents.htm

FOR KIDS

Kids Help Phone 1-800-668-6868
www.kidshelpphone.ca

NAME IT 2 CHANGE IT COMMUNITY
CAMPAIGN AGAINST BULLYING
    101 Nanticoke Creek Parkway, Box 5054
    Townsend, ON N0A 1S0
    1-800-265-8087 ext. 263
www.nameit2changeit.ca

STOP CYBER BULLYING
www.stopcyberbullying.org

PACER CENTER'S KIDS AGAINST BULLYING
    8161 Normandale Blvd.,
    Bloomington, MN 53437
    952-838-9000
www.pacerkidsagainstbullying.org
www.pacerteensagainstbullying.org

WHERE PEACE LIVES
    PO Box 2007
    Red Bank, NJ 07701
www.WherePeaceLives.org

FOR TEACHERS

Davis, Julia and Davis, Stan.
Schools Where Everyone Belongs.
Champaign: Research Press, 2005

Garbarino, James and deLara, Ellen.
*And Words Can Hurt Forever:
How To Protect Adolescents From Bullying,
Harassment and Emotional Violence.*
New York: Free Press, 2003

Parsons, Les.
Bullied Teacher: Bullied Student.
Markham: Pembroke Publishers, 2005

Philips, Rick, Linney, John and Pack, Chris.
*Safe School Ambassadors: Harnessing
Student Power to Stop Bullying and
Violence.*
San Francisco: Jossey-Bass, 2008

PEACEFUL SCHOOLS INTERNATIONAL,
PO Box 660, Annapolis Royal, NS
B0S 1A0
902-532-1111
www.peacefulschoolsinternational.org
1-866-532-0228
(toll free anywhere in North America)

ROOTS OF EMPATHY
250 Ferrand Dr., Suite 800, Toronto,
ON M3C 3G8
416-944-3001
www.rootsofempathy.org

SAIDAT MUSIC, MOVEMENT AND
MOTIVATION TO ELIMINATE BULLYING
www.saidat.ca

SAFE CHILD PROGRAM
c/o Coalition for Children
PO Box 6304
Denver, CO 80206
www.safechild.org

INDEX